ENDORSEMENTS

I have known Dr. Jinwright personally for more than twenty years. His ministry has always been at the cutting edge of evangelism, forever moving the church of God out of traditions that are often dry and fruitless. In the center of his message is the call to reveal what God is saying to His people, and the available spiritual power to accomplish the goals set before us.

This book flows out of a committed and intellectual mind that is alive in the fullness of God's Spirit. Dr. Jinwright has a powerful passion to lift up the church of Jesus Christ. *Rise Up* is a must-read for all who seek genuine Christian renewal for the church of God in our times.

—Harold A. Carter, Senior Pastor
New Shiloh Baptist Church
Baltimore, Maryland

Dr. Anthony Jinwright has written the premier book on the power of the anointed life. *Rise Up* is not a book of theory, but a book about the preparation of every individual who carries God's message into the everyday world. It equips us all to get extraordinary results in our personal walk with God.

If you love the Lord, this book is for you. If you want to be a better witness, this book is for you. If you are looking for a miracle in your life or ministry, this book is for you! Applause for Dr. Jinwright for writing a book that will make better believers and better churches.

—Dr. Frank M. Reid III, Senior Pastor
Bethel African Methodist Episcopal Church
Baltimore, Maryland

In a style uniquely his own, Dr. Anthony Jinwright provides clarion insight and prophetic summons to the prerequisite ingredients of consecration and anointing as the foundation of impactful ministry. *Rise Up* is necessary reading for every disciple whose prayer is to be submitted to God's will and plan for twenty-first century ministry.

—Bishop Harold Calvin Ray, Senior Pastor
Redemptive Life Fellowship Church
West Palm Beach, Florida
Founder and CEO
National Center for Faith-Based Initiative

Rise Up is an intriguing faith journey of a man of faith who stands on the center's edge of ministry and shares his calling as a preacher.

—Dr. Clifford A. Jones, Sr., Senior Pastor
Friendship Missionary Baptist Church
Charlotte, North Carolina

RISE UP

Breaking Free into Anointed Living

RISE UP

Breaking Free into Anointed Living

Dr. Anthony L. Jinwright

ധ
WHITAKER
HOUSE

RISE UP

Dr. Anthony L. Jinwright
Greater Salem Church
5318 Salem Church Road
Charlotte, NC 28216
Phone: 704.399.5448 • Fax: 704.392.3670

ISBN: 0-88368-760-7
Printed in the United States of America
© 2002 by Dr. Anthony Jinwright

Whitaker House
30 Hunt Valley Circle
New Kensington, PA 15068
Visit our web site at: www.whitakerhouse.com

Library of Congress Cataloging-in-Publication Data

Jinwright, Anthony, 1956–
 Rise up / by Anthony Jinwright.
 p. cm.
Includes bibliographical references.
 ISBN 0-88368-760-7 (pbk. : alk. paper)
 1. Anointing of the Holy Spirit. I. Title.
BT123 .J56 2002
243—dc21   2002004500

1 2 3 4 5 6 7 8 9 10 11 12 / 09 08 07 06 05 04 03 02

CONTENTS

FOREWORD

GOD WANTS TO SHAKE THINGS UP

You're a Christian. Do you know why? What's it all about? You are trying to be like Jesus—a gentle man who tried to teach people to be nice to each other, right?

Wrong! If your biggest spiritual goal is to be a nice person—if the Golden Rule is your most powerful idea of love—you are standing in a good place. And good is the eternal enemy of the best.

Jesus said, *"I have come that they may have life, and have it to the full"* (John 10:10 NIV). He died and rose from the dead to win us an eternal, anointed life of supernatural impact. We need to believe that, and live like we believe it! Too many Christians are convinced that their words and actions—their lives—don't count for much. After all, what can one little person do?

Let me tell you about a man known as the British bulldog. He wasn't a soldier, and he wasn't a special agent. His biggest talent was for argument, and his hobby was painting. This man saved a nation, and perhaps the free world, from being ground under the jackboots of Nazi storm troopers.

It was the darkest of days. The gloom of war hung over the United Kingdom like a dark shroud of death. France had fallen to the Nazi armies. The German blitzkrieg had decimated Allied resistance and chased the British forces off the European mainland. Only the miracle evacuation of her shattered army at Dunkirk saved England from total defeat. Now the battle for Britain raged. German bombers pummeled the key cities of England, blasting military and civilian targets alike. London was in ruins. The English people clung to their slim hopes as they prepared for the inevitable Nazi invasion. Critical wartime supplies were running low. American support, although appreciated, was not sufficient for the task. England felt very alone.

It was 1939. Sir Winston Churchill, the newly appointed prime minister, decided to address Parliament. That day, Churchill gave his most famous speech to the English nation. The message was carried on national radio, and Churchill was at his best. With a torrent of fiery rhetoric, he rallied the despondent Brits out of their despair. He kindled hope and determination against the Nazi juggernaut. He was determined that the British would fight the enemy with all their strength, even if it meant bloody combat on the shores of Dover or in the streets of London. They would never give up—never! The hope of Western civilization hung in the balance, and England would rise to face its greatest challenge.

Churchill's speech scored a direct hit on the will and nerve of his nation. The British people, from the top brass and titular royalty down to the dockworkers in Liverpool and coal miners in Wales, were galvanized in will and spirit to go on with the fight. The heart of a nation was revived in one night! The people had hope!

Little did Churchill know the ultimate impact of his speech. That same night, in Berlin, Adolph Hitler listened intently to a translated version of the address. The words and heart of Churchill came through to the Führer. In fact, Hitler was so impressed by the declaration of gall and grit that he decided to postpone the invasion of England. He turned his attention to the Eastern front and launched an ill-fated attack on his former ally, Stalinist Russia.

Across the Atlantic Ocean, another pair of interested ears tuned in to Churchill's address. President Franklin Roosevelt had been struggling for weeks to decide whether the United States should step up its support of Britain. The English were not impressive in the first years of the Second World War. Political and military blunders created the impression that England was a lost cause. Roosevelt was not sure if it would be worth sinking more American resources into a losing effort. As the president drank in the words of the prime minister, his reservations melted away in the white heat of Churchill's passionate rhetoric. Roosevelt became a believer in Britain. Within weeks, increased convoys of Liberty ships would set sail to England to replenish critical supplies. That night, the words of Winston Churchill turned the tide of World War II (adapted from Peter Hume, *The Language of Leadership*).

All words have incredible power. The proper phrase, spoken at the right time, can alter the course of lives, institutions, and even nations. Throughout history, effective leaders have used persuasive speech to their advantage. Yet the impact of human discourse, no matter how eloquent, cannot compare with the power and impact of God's Word, whether it is spoken with authority or lived quietly. This is the anointed life Jesus calls you to—logic on fire, unique communication empowered and energized by the Spirit of God. Throughout redemptive history, God's people have led through the anointed proclamation of the Word and through lives of integrity. Will you?

ALL WORDS HAVE INCREDIBLE POWER.

Revival at Harvard!

The American church faced dark years immediately following the Revolutionary War. Church attendance dwindled to an estimated 10 percent of the population! Civility was dying, and public behavior was often drunken and lewd. Educational institutions, originally founded by the church, became enamored with the European Enlightenment. Free thinking and atheist societies were promoted among the student bodies. At Harvard, a school originally established as a training ground for Puritan clergy, barely a believer could be found. In the midst of this irreligious academic community, Harvard's president, Timothy Dwight, began preaching during the chapel services. His messages hit home and triggered a period of revival among the students, turning around the institutional life of this prestigious school and, eventually, the fledgling nation!

All it took to revive a generation of Americans was one man who passionately refused to accept the darkness around him. This powerful life of anointing is not reserved for a few elect individuals in scattered areas of revival. God intends it for you! He desires to set the whole earth ablaze with the knowledge of His love. His glory yearns to break forth through a thousand firestorms sparked by the intensity of uncompromising believers. When the Lord wants to shake things up, He sends people with anointed lives. He sends people who share His vision. He sends you!

This call is an awesome privilege. The same divine Word that called the worlds into existence and decreed the saving counsel of salvation thunders from the lives and lips of God's servants. The Word has sublime power. Biblical tradition and the history of the church confirm the potency of God's truth. As the Word has been spoken, hearers have encountered God, summoned by His sovereign and saving will.

In the Old Testament, God used the voices of His prophets as well as the strong arms of judges like Samson. As God's "covenant enforcers," they both beckoned a wayward Israel to faithfulness and took up arms against her enemies (Fee 1993, 165–167). Sometimes God used His servants to warn of coming judgment, as He did with Samuel, Jonah, and Amos. In gracious counterpoint, He often used the same people to call Israel to a merciful Lord and to an active hope in His proffered salvation. When Yahweh's servants acted in divine might, lives were changed and nations chastened.

The centrality of God's messengers continues in the New Testament. Jesus was the supreme herald of God. He was uniquely set apart by the Holy Spirit to speak God's message (Luke 4:14; John 3:34). His were the words of eternal life (John 6:68). His life conveyed unique power and authority. Jesus could restore a profligate prostitute, raise the dead, and cast out a legion of demons. This legacy of anointing extended through the apostles and other believers whose message turned the Roman Empire upside down. It continues to this day, and He wants it to be active in your life.

THE VISION OF THIS BOOK

Rise Up is a book about profound change. The agent of change is the Spirit of Christ working through the Word of God. His work is more than a facelift; it is a deep and radical transformation of our daily lives. I am a witness to the revolutionary ways God can work. I know that the anointing changes human hearts—and whole communities. My own life's journey will illustrate the process. God has patiently worked in me to build a life empowered by the Spirit, and I speak with the humble and simple conviction that my metamorphosis was engineered by our sovereign and gracious Lord.

THE WORK OF THE SPIRIT IS A RADICAL TRANSFORMATION.

As I have sought to be an anointed vessel, I have learned some key principles and spiritual dynamics to foster and enhance a successful Christian walk. The steps are relatively simple. They are meant to prepare the messenger as well as the message. As Dennis Kinlaw puts it,

> The greatest problem in preaching is not the preparation of the sermon but the preparation of the preacher. We have an abundance of books and a raft of seminary courses on how to prepare and deliver a sermon; but scarcely anyone tells how to get ourselves ready to do the preaching that God calls us to do (1985, 17).

This book is intended for the spiritual formation of those in the church. If you truly seek to follow after Christ, you will be living out the message of hope, to be read by the people around you. As a result, I may use the terms *preacher, messenger,* and *believer* interchangeably. Don't get confused—I'm talking about you! At times I will address issues of pulpit style and sermon content (I am, after all, a pastor and preacher), but my passionate concern is for all believers to rise to a new level of relationship with the Holy Spirit. It does not matter if you are in a mainline or free-church tradition; the principles in this book will work. Whether you are a vocational minister or a lay believer, God wants to ignite a fire of passion and hope in your heart. There are groves of books providing an education in Christianity. I pray that *Rise Up* will touch your heart and spirit, and help you to soar.

In the following chapters you will discover how to:

• Understand the Holy Spirit's anointing and experience it in your daily life

• Draw on the Spirit's anointing to energize your life

• Discover how God can guide and enrich your quiet times by "partnering with the Holy Spirit"

• Translate your sense of divine calling into God-ordained spiritual authority

• Promote new covenant principles of liberation and transformation with your speech—and your life

• Transform your greatest struggles into opportunities to share Christ

• Employ the concept of "divine alignment" to walk in unity and faith with fellow believers and your church

• Defuse satanic opposition and optimize the impact of God's Word

The book is based around these principles, and I want to invite you to read with an open and hungry heart. God is getting ready to shake things up, and you are called to be a part of the action! May the Lord use these pages to rekindle spiritual passion and power in your life so that you can *Rise Up!*

SPECIAL
ACKNOWLEDGMENTS

This work would not have been possible without the love and support of my faithful and loyal co-laborer in ministry, my wife, Harriet Porter-Jinwright. You have always been my number one fan, and I praise God daily for you.

To my loving daughter, Anthonae (Toni), better known as "all I got!" Daddy's courage and strength are renewed every time I think of you. My prayer of thanksgiving to God includes the precious gift He gave us in you.

To my friends and colleagues in ministry who have helped me to sharpen my tools in the enterprise of kingdom building, many thanks. Had it not been for your wisdom and unparalleled expertise, much of what I have achieved would not have been accomplished.

To Dr. Steven W. Klipowicz, my friend and contributing editor. Thank you for the countless hours you spent listening to and aiding me in transforming the passions of my heart into this chronicle of my journey.

Words cannot express my appreciation to the administrative team at Greater Salem Church for working tirelessly beyond the call of responsibility to assist me in this project.

And to the faithful congregants of Greater Salem Church, I thank God for you. Across the years, you have given me the privilege and the latitude to soar as the Spirit of the Lord directed. Never have you tried to hinder me from doing whatever was in my heart to do for the kingdom's sake. To you I dedicate this labor of love.

Then, I give all praise to God for empowering me to persevere in spite of the odds. Without the constant presence of the Holy Spirit reviving me and igniting me to keep going, the pen and pad would never have met to fill the pages with the message within this book. God, I love You and bless You with my whole heart!

—Dr. Anthony L. Jinwright

CHAPTER ONE

GET INTO THE GAME

GET INTO THE GAME

We live in an age that desperately needs revival. North American Christianity has endured more than two decades of continual decline. In 1975, *Time* magazine proclaimed the "Year of the Evangelical." Since then, the vitality and influence of the church has slid continually downward. Present Sunday church attendance, historically a stable statistic, is at the lowest point in thirty years. According to researcher George Barna, the average Protestant church has lost 10 percent in Sunday attendance in the last seven years (Barna 1996, 36–37)! Less than 35 percent of Americans attend church on any given weekend. The presence of young adults has slipped even more. Of those thirty and under, fewer than 15 percent attend church. Mainline church participation has eroded the most. The Episcopal Church alone has lost one-third of its members in the last two decades! Evangelical and Pentecostal groups, who enjoyed great success in the 1970s, ebbed in a number of key indicators during the decade of the 1990s.

These downturns in church attendance are linked to other significant trends. Sunday school, as an institution, is struggling for life. Knowledge of biblical truth and Christian doctrine has evaporated from the pews. Charitable giving to Christian ministries, another reliable indicator of religious commitment, has been sluggish despite the greatest economic upswing in American history (Barna 1996, 111). These are symptomatic of the growing lack of religious commitment among the general population—during a period when interest in all kinds of spirituality has been growing! A national crisis of religious faith may be looming. Pollster George Gallup hits at the casual approach Americans take to faith:

> While religion is highly popular in America, it is to a large extent superficial; it does not change people's lives to the degree one would expect from the level of professed faith (1989, 48).

At the heart of this decline, according to Wade Clark Roof, is a loss of our deepest loyalties:

> At the core of the problem, as many believers see it, is a crisis of commitment: people do not take seriously their vows, their duties, and their obligations—to others and to God (1993, 67).

In the last two decades, believers have scurried to respond to the crisis. Concerts of prayer, an emphasis on fasting and spiritual growth, prayer walking, renewal movements such as Promise Keepers, and strategic ventures like Mission 2000 have been produced as partial antidotes to the growing religious lethargy. Fads have come and gone, and creative models have emerged, challenging local congregations to become relevant to dynamic cultural and demographic shifts. In a quest for innovative solutions, some churches are trying to be more adept at interfacing with the emerging post-Christian age. Congregations, in order to be successful, are becoming more purpose-driven, seeker-sensitive, or relevant to a particular niche in the prevailing demographic analyses.

In spite of these energetic endeavors, the average Christian still struggles to keep himself engaged and growing, let alone impact the community around him.

Undoubtedly, the local church needs to be reengineered. Tradition-bound congregations can be hopelessly out of step with the needs of our world. Changes need to be made, but changes in church structure and philosophy of ministry deal only with surface issues. Deep-rooted and lasting change in the hearts of individuals is required. Radical renewal is called for, but only one orchestrated by the Holy Spirit will make a significant difference.

THE AVERAGE CHRISTIAN STILL STRUGGLES TO KEEP GROWING.

SITTING ON THE SIDELINES

Unfortunately, biblical theology rarely plays a dominant role in how we actually "do" Christianity. Biblical metaphors sound wonderful in church mission statements, but practical factors are what drive our daily practice of religion. Be honest: Do you feel like an organ in the supernatural body of Christ, or more like a member of the theater society? How many times have you evaluated your service, and your church services, as performances instead of encounters with ultimate Truth?

Now imagine the perspective of the minister:

Today's time-pressured, attention-challenged saints offer special challenges! As eternal truths of glory are pronounced from the pulpit, the congregation fidgets in the morass of mundane life. Kids wiggle, sleep-deprived adults snore while cell phones beep—all a reminder that the sermon is an interruption in the flow of real life. Kick-off is at one, and restaurants get crowded past noon. What can the preacher expect?

No one expects much more from the sermon than a few inspirational thoughts and brevity. The message is often reduced to a "sermonette," wedged into a morning crowded with worship, announcements, baby dedications, and numerous other "essential" events. Topics are trimmed down to the felt needs of not only the congregation, but also the visitor. Theological concepts are jettisoned and any Bible references reduced to what can fit on a bulletin-sized sermon guide or PowerPoint slide.

In fact, the Word of Truth has become increasingly marginal in the life of the modern believer. The more we demand convenient, user-friendly, and seeker-sensitive Christianity, the more God speaks from the sidelines and not the center of our lives.

Even worse than the things that crowd out God's truth are the lies that too many Christians have believed. For over fifty years, many scholars have pushed the idea that the Bible is human literature to be subjectively understood and interpreted. The heart of this scholarship mocks the conviction of objective truth, claiming that the meaning of the biblical text is simply what it means to you. These ideas are no longer confined to academia—they have oozed into the consciousness of the common people. As a result, the typical person questions all claims to authoritative truth. In fact, 50 percent of professing Christians no longer hold to the idea of absolute truth (Barna 2002, 59–60).

Has this emerging cultural consensus on truth drained your expectation of receiving an authoritative message from God? Instead of living out of conviction regarding what "thus saith the Lord," do you muddle along with a "personal" perspective on the biblical text? A messenger pronounces the truth; he doesn't merely "share." The loss of an authoritative Word will gut the soul of biblical living. As Haddon Robinson puts it, most Christians abandon the authority of the Scriptures, confronting others not with a word from God, but with just another idea from men: "Therefore, most [Christian living] evokes little more than a wide yawn. God is not in it" (1980, 18).

Do our lives flow from Christ as the divine center, or do we speak from the sidelines of personal opinion? No wonder music and special programs are claiming the lion's share of church time. Even contemporary worshippers prefer the mellow mood generated by the choir or praise team over the confrontational edge and embarrassment of objective and authoritative preaching. Is it any wonder we've been buried by an ungodly culture?

THE CALL TO RISE UP

Is there a cure for the spiritual malaise of our day? Is there a balm in Gilead (Jeremiah 8:22)? Although the problems facing Christians are complex, the solution is simple: a recovery of the anointed life. Energized, divinely directed living is a potent antidote to the paralysis of discouragement that is immobilizing many believers! Our survival depends on making the Word primary, but the supernatural anointing of the Spirit is vital to making the message an agent of radical transformation. Remember, when God wants to shake things up, He sends anointed believers.

GOD WILL EQUIP YOU WITH THE POWER TO FULFILL HIS CALL.

How about you? Have you been sitting on the sidelines too long? Have you given up hope that your life can be more than a religious "trip to the gym" on Sunday mornings? Do you hunger for God to do something new? Then, Christian, God is calling you to rise up!

First of all, you must rise up in God. The anointed life demands an awareness of divine calling and potency. Change begins with you! You have to have the goods, whether you're in a pew, a cubicle, or the pulpit. You must let God's Spirit ratchet up your passion to a whole new level. This requires a deep and intimate relationship with Him. You may be able to recite and explain large sections of Scripture, but that's not enough. You won't improve your life or anyone else's without the

Spirit working the Word into people's hearts. When the Spirit's internal revelation breaks into people's lives, it has the potential for radically transforming them (Kinlaw 1985, 4).

Now is the time to make the Holy Spirit your partner. Without Him, you won't be effective. With Him, you will soar to new heights.

Second, rise up in your own eyes! Most Christians need to have their self-image renovated. You have been called by God to be an agent of change—to glow like a spiritual nuclear meltdown! God will equip you with the authority and power you need to fulfill His call on your life. He has chosen you to do more than provide neat self-help talks to your friends. You have been called to present a "Word from on high." The Christian experience is not a form of spiritual entertainment. It is an encounter with the living God and a demonstration of divine power! Humble yourself before the Lord, and let Him lift you up. A reborn believer will connect the world to the power of God.

God is among His people. He is present and desires to make Himself known. Our very bodies are the temples of the Holy Spirit, and the absence of anointed living is a key indicator that we have lost touch with the essential nature of the Christian life as the dwelling place of God by His Spirit.

In the American church's desire to relate to our culture, we are in danger of "dumbing down" our awareness of the supernatural aspect of corporate life and faith (Dawn 1995). The call to reformation will fall only on deaf ears unless believers like you hunger for an anointed life! Without the anointed life, the church functions more as a social club, not the dwelling place of the Lord. No one expects anything exciting to happen—no wonder the typical congregation member regularly misses church.

This gnawing dissatisfaction with the institutional church was captured by Frederick Buechner in an article entitled "Theologian Reflects on Pals and Prophets in Pulpit," published in the *Richmond Times-Dispatch,* 20 April 1996:

> For many years now I have taken to going to church less and less because I find so little there of what I hunger for. It is the presence of God that I hunger for.

Does your place in the church more closely resemble a membership with the Rotary club than a dynamic part of the house of God? Do you hunger for the authentic presence of the living God? Then you must take the steps needed to restore the priority of your own relationship with God. Nothing can replace genuine personal worship. It challenges, stimulates, and motivates us to become more like our God. This type of worship transforms us. It can come only from God. Worship without God's leading is empty of meaning and power. Christians need a genuine experience of God, not more time sitting under stained-glass windows listening to the impoverished horizons of human creativity.

One pastor told the newspaper that his church is popular because of noteworthy celebrities who attend. He was delighted that prominent politicians, professional athletes, and other well-known personalities came to his church. As I read this article, my heart sank. My dismay was not a result of professional jealousy. It was a result of spiritual jealousy. I am jealous for Jesus. When I hear of a growing church I simply ask, "Is Jesus being exalted?" Jesus said, *"And I, if I be lifted up...will draw all men unto me"* (John 12:32). Do people leave the church saying, "I had an encounter with Jesus," or do they leave saying, "I had a chance to meet the mayor"?

When Jesus is lifted up, God comes down to interact with His people. When the messengers are Christ-centered, lives are changed. Christians must transform the culture, never accommodate to it, and that won't happen in fifty minutes on Sunday mornings. This can be done only from the standpoint of a vital encounter with the living God. As Sally Morgenthaler puts it:

> The hour we spend at services like these will most likely be glutted with polished performances and pedestal personalities. Our emotions will be tapped by well-planned musical sequences and segues, culturally correct humor, pithy anecdotes, and well-rehearsed humility. We will have our brains stuffed with information about how to make life work and how to work harder at life. Most likely, we will leave feeling good about our-selves. But one thing we will not have done: We will not meet with God. A true encounter with God leaves us with a lot more than good feelings. It leaves us with changed hearts and calls us to changed lives. Very simply, to experience God's presence is to be transformed from the inside out (1995, 135).

God wants to do something new for you. He wants to transform you from the inside out. You must not value the Word of God at a distance any longer. The Coach ARE YOU READY has blown His whistle and is signaling TO BE ENTIRELY for you to get off the bench and into TRANSFORMED? the game. You are central in His game plan for the church. Are you ready for a change? Are you willing to answer the call to action? The following chapters will guide you into the reality of an anointed life. Ask the Spirit to open your heart and life to a fresh encounter with Him. I repeat: When God wants to shake things up, He sends anointed believers! May your heart's cry be, "Lord, send me."

QUESTIONS FOR REFLECTION AND DISCUSSION

1. Recall one time in which you felt God really used your words or life to make an impact. Describe what that experience did for you and those who heard your words.

2. What does it mean to you to be anointed with the Holy Spirit? Describe a significant time you experienced God's anointing.

3. If you were really to "rise up" in your life, how would things have to change in your relationship with God, with your family? How would your part in the church need to change? What are your reservations about fully pursuing these changes?

THE SPIRITUAL REALITY OF THE ANOINTING

THE SPIRITUAL REALITY OF THE ANOINTING

Oh, Lord, give Thy servant this mornin' the eyes of the eagle and the wisdom of the owl; connect his soul with the gospel telephone in the central skies; 'luminate his brow with the Sun of Heaven; possess his mind with love for the people; turpentine his imagination, grease his lips with 'possum oil, loosen his tongue with the sledgehammer of thy power; 'lectrify his brain with the lightnin' of the word; put 'petual motion on his arms; fill him plum full of the dynamite of Thy glory; 'noint him all over with the kerosene oil of Thy salvation and set him on fire. Amen!
—Kenneth McFarland

THE QUEST FOR SPIRITUAL POWER

Living according to God's Word requires His power. Unless your silent message is one of divine life, witnessing is a futile and ineffectual waste of time—in

33

the same way that, most of the time, lifeless preaching isn't even entertaining. Sadly, many Christians are unaware of the power of God's Spirit. They fail to see how it could revolutionize their approach to life. They are like the seasoned woodsman who was accustomed to cutting timber the traditional way, with his manual handsaw. He had no use for "newfangled" technology. But when a local hardware shopkeeper told him of a power saw that could cut ten cords of wood per day, the aging woodsman decided to give it a try. The next day the woodsman returned to the hardware store, tired, still dirty, and visibly upset. "You said this thing would cut ten cords of wood a day," he told the shopkeeper. "I worked till I was blue in the face but could cut only one." "That can't be," replied the shopkeeper. "Let's see what the problem is." He took the power saw, inspected it closely, then flipped the power switch and gave the starter cord a hearty pull. Its twin-valved engine roared to life. The startled woodsman jumped a little and asked, "What's that noise?"

There needs to be a divine awareness in your everyday life. Have you made the connection? Until you do, you will be "sawing" in your own strength. You will never bear the fruit of the Spirit without the anointing of God. Spiritually effective living can't come from your own efforts. It is the gift of God, who creates life out of nothing.

In his perceptive book, *The Soul of Ministry,* Ray Anderson says that all ministry is really the ministry of God through us. We can never do it by ourselves. God ministers *ex nihilo.* This Latin phrase means literally, "out of nothing." He creates life out of nothing. The

Creation narrative in Genesis and the biblical examples of Abram and Moses underscore this truth. The abysmal void of pre-creation, the barrenness of Abram and Sarai, and the absurdity of a refugee nomad commanding ancient Egypt's Pharaoh to "let my people go"—all demand a power that can be answered only by God's creative activity. In fact, the blessing of God presupposes our weakness and barrenness! It is when we are at our emptiest that the work of God can be genuinely appreciated.

This is the starting point of the anointing—the unshakable conviction that only God can produce His work in you. Only He can create life in dead, barren hearts. The Christian's sense of personal powerlessness is the vital seedbed for the anointing of God. In humble faith, rely solely on God to bless you through your barrenness. You are not sufficient for your calling. You are not adequate to carry God's message in the manner it should be proclaimed. Get that through to your fragile ego, if you have one. Only the Lord can create *ex nihilo*. In the void of your heart, the Word and the Spirit must blaze with the light of the Second Creation (2 Corinthians 4:6). The transforming Word comes only from God.

WHAT IS THE STARTING POINT OF THE ANOINTING?

THE SPIRITUAL LIFE AS A DIVINE WORK

God is the source of all life. Spiritual reformation not only relies on the life-giving words of God, but it is actually an activity of God. We are called to be the messengers and agents of God (1 Peter 4:11). He works through us! As God the third person, the Holy Spirit provides supernatural insight and wisdom to the Christian, but the believer must listen and obey. "True [spiritual life] from start to finish is the work of the Holy Spirit. It is God seeking us and finding us" (Knox 1957, 46). The Spirit desires to attend to the sum total of life. Learn to trust Him. He yearns to guide and empower from beginning to end.

The Spirit will reveal to you the first glimmers of truth in your biblical study and sharing. He can clarify what prayer-soaked direction you need to take. His presence can embolden you to make good decisions. Finally, He will apply the life-giving Word to your **BEGIN TO NURTURE** heart. Through it all, the Spirit is at **AN INTIMATE** work. He is the creative master of the **RELATIONSHIP WITH** whole process. This is not automatic. **THE HOLY SPIRIT.** As a junior partner, the Christian must nurture an intimate relationship with the Holy Spirit. You have to be in touch with, and open to, Him. This includes a willingness on your part to totally rely on the Lord's direction.

The apostle Paul clearly held this understanding of his life's purpose:

> *We proclaim him, admonishing and teaching everyone with all wisdom, so that we may **present** everyone **perfect in Christ**. To this end I labor, struggling with all his energy, which so powerfully works in me.*
> (Colossians 1:28–29, emphasis added)

Paul knew his work was a calling of God. Radically conceived, it was an activity of God accomplished through Paul by God's power. The word for *"energy"* in this passage is used in the New Testament only to describe supernatural power. Paul clearly understood that the power in his life was supernatural (Bromiley 1985, under "energeis"). Therefore, living in Christ is an activity that is God-ordained, God-directed, and God-energized!

Has it ever dawned on you that your daily walk could be directed and empowered by the Lord? The apostle recognized that he was working with God in his preaching and teaching. The same can be true for you. The key is intimacy with the Holy Spirit.

THE PERSON OF THE HOLY SPIRIT

How can a Christian experience the supernatural power of God? The answer is found through the Holy Spirit. The theological and practical foundations for anointed living rest upon the Holy Spirit. The Spirit and the Word of God are the divine agents of creation and redemption. Each is needed in the day-to-day Christian life. The Holy Spirit is more than a divine influence or power. He is the third person of the Trinity, fully God. As God, the Holy Spirit is supremely personal. He is a person, not a force. As a divine person, the Spirit shares all the characteristics of the Godhead and all the qualities we expect from a true person. Since He is divine, the Spirit is omnipresent, omnipotent, and omniscient. As fully personal, the Spirit has an intellect, emotions, and a will. Because He is a personal deity, I can experience the Spirit of Jesus in a relationship. We communicate with each other. He speaks to me and I listen. I speak to Him and He hears me when I pray. It is my relationship with the Spirit of Jesus that forms the fountainhead of my Christian life. Abiding in Christ is the essential pre-condition of bearing genuine spiritual fruit for God (John 15:1–16). The profound secret of the anointing is awesomely simple: intimacy with the Spirit of the Lord.

As a pastor, I draw on the personal reality of the Spirit as the wellspring of life and the executive force in my ministry of the Word. Since only God can create *ex nihilo* (out of nothing), I must rely totally on the Spirit's direction and anointing. Preaching, like the rest of life, must be a partnership with God's Spirit. Charles Haddon Spurgeon, called the Prince of Preachers, had to ascend fifteen steps to his pulpit. As he climbed up the rounded stairway to preach, it is said that he muttered to himself on each step, "I believe in the Holy Ghost" (Stott 1982, 334). Fifteen times this giant among preachers confessed his total dependency on the third person of the Trinity. Should our sense of dependency on the Spirit be any less?

Intimacy with God does not excuse you from being under His lordship. A personal relationship with the Spirit of Jesus must never become a common thing. Respect and obedience are essential. Jesus is the true Shepherd. Even as a pastor, I am just an under-shepherd serving a small part of His immense flock (John 10:1–18; 1 Peter 5:1–4). Following His leadership is critical to spiritual success, no matter who you are.

Do you know what the Lord wants to say through you in any given week? What does God want to do in your character today? Too often, Christians don't see the bigger picture—they see only themselves. Jesus sees all the sheep. He recognizes that some are ill, some are hungry, and others are in danger of straying. He alone has a heavenly perspective, so He alone is qualified to lead you into the anointing.

Your career path should align with the emerging purposes the Lord has for your life. Similarly, your response to people at home must show both the mercy and strength of character that Jesus modeled. In this sense, simply living becomes strategic. Your witness should be formative—that is, it must be an instrument in God's hand for the salvation and encouragement of those around you. This is possible only when you let the Spirit of Jesus do the diagnosis. Jesus has a clear vision of every situation. He can pinpoint the conditions of all kinds of people, and the steps needed to reach them (Revelation 2–3). This wisdom and insight will come to you through partnering with the Holy Spirit.

SIMPLY LIVING CAN BE STRATEGIC.

WHAT IS THE ANOINTING?

Partnering with the Holy Spirit recognizes that the heart of the Christian life is the power of God. This calls for a rebirth of intimacy. God intends personal reformation to be the fuel for the fires of worldwide revival! The biblical message, demonstrated in a life of integrity and the power of the Holy Spirit, will draw people. A message like that challenges, convicts, and consecrates those who see it.

The anointing has such a powerful impact that it should be coveted by every child of God. The great preachers of the church have understood that success hinges on the sovereign supernatural activity of the

Holy Spirit. This is what C. H. Spurgeon called "the sacred anointing." There isn't a textbook definition of the term *anointing*. It is a concept with deep biblical roots and a rich heritage among the giants of faith. Unfortunately, most Christians don't understand or appreciate the potential of the anointing. If the anointing is so crucial, then what is it?

Anointing in the Old Testament

The actual word *anointing* (*massah*, Hebrew) reflects the Old Testament custom of consecrating things to God through the application of sacred oil. Moses was commanded to formulate a special oil of anointing according to God's instructions (Exodus 30:22–25). This fragrant mixture was used to anoint the tabernacle, its furnishings, and its personnel (vv. 26–33). The oil of anointing was unique and used only for sacred purposes such as consecrating ministers. Aaron and his sons were set apart for priestly service through anointing with this oil. God ordered Israel's kings to be anointed with the same oil. This sacred oil identified the true king of God's people (1 Kings 1:39). Prophets were also anointed with the sacred oil (1 Kings 19:16). Anointing with oil was the outward sign of authority for all true servants of Yahweh. It indicated divine selection and empowerment for a specific role (1 Samuel 16:13). No servant of the Lord was considered qualified without the holy anointing (Oldford 1998, 215).

In the Old Testament, the concept of anointing combined calling, consecration, and empowerment. Over time the Hebrew terms for *consecration* and *anointing* were used interchangeably in reference to a "setting apart" for God's use (Oldford 1998, 216–217). Even the heathen King Cyrus of Persia could be God's anointed servant (Isaiah 45:1)! The prophets told of a time when the remnant of Israel would be anointed, not with oil, but with the Spirit, to enable it to become a light to the nations (Isaiah 42:1–4; 49:6). Eventually, *anointing* and *calling* became synonymous.

The prophetic hopes of the old covenant rested upon God's promise to restore Israel under the reign of a coming Son of David. This Branch of the root of Jesse would be an anointed servant of Yahweh, and the anointing would be an endowment of power and wisdom through the Holy Spirit of God (Isaiah 11:2).

> *"As for me, this is my covenant with them," says the LORD. "My Spirit, who is on you, and my words that I have put in your mouth will not depart from your mouth, or from the mouths of your children, or from the mouths of their descendants from this time on and forever," says the LORD.*
> (Isaiah 59:21 NIV; also see Acts 2:32–34)

Many prophets delivered messages on this theme of restoration and anointing. Joel predicted that, in the final days, a corporate anointing would rest upon the restored people of God, and all would be anointed to speak God's Word as prophets (Joel 2:28–29). Are you ready to have the power of God working through you in this way?

ANOINTING IN THE NEW TESTAMENT

The Hebrews' cherished hopes of the anointed Son of David were fulfilled in Jesus "the Christ" (from the Greek *christos*—"the anointed one"). At the synagogue in Nazareth, He identified Himself as the anointed servant foretold by Isaiah (Luke 4:18–19). At the shore of the Jordan River, during His baptism, Jesus was anointed with the Holy Spirit and confirmed by God as the messianic Son of David (Luke 3:21–22). At that point, He was anointed with the power to do good and liberate those who were oppressed by the devil (Acts 10:38). The embodiment of anointing now rested in one person: Jesus, the true messianic Son of David.

Through Jesus' death, resurrection, and ascension, He was enthroned at the right hand of the Father as both Christ and Lord (Acts 2:36). From this position of glory, the Anointed One poured out the promise of the Father—the baptism of the Holy Spirit (v. 33). The church as the corporate body of Christ was birthed on the Day of Pentecost, when the body of Christ was anointed with the Spirit of God as a demonstration of its calling, consecration, and empowerment for service. The servants of the Gospel experienced God's dynamic and miraculous support to attest to the truth they proclaimed. The whole church continued the ministry of the anointed Christ as His body and people (Acts 1:1, 14). God's people were called by the Spirit's anointing to function as prophets, priests, and royal heirs. The Spirit's anointing rested on the church in its totality and upon each member specifically, for each believer received the promise of the Father. Every believer was anointed by God (2 Corinthians 1:21), and each Christian had a residual anointing through the indwelling Spirit of God (1 John 2:20, 27). The anointing testified that every Christian is called by God, consecrated as a saint, and gifted by the Spirit for specific ministry and service to the church and the world (1 Corinthians 1:21; 12:7).

LIVING IN THE ANOINTING

This biblical background provides a useful perspective on how God anoints and empowers those He calls. Throughout the history of the church, Christians have identified a unique and specific work of God on and through men and women whom He has called. This effect has been called "unction," or anointing. When the anointing was present on a preacher, both he and his audience sensed a divine accompaniment to the message. What this anointing is more generally, and how it works, will be discussed next.

THE ANOINTING ENABLES YOU TO BE SPIRITUALLY EFFECTIVE.

The following definition highlights the key aspects of this concept:

The anointing is a special, sovereign activity of the Holy Spirit that accompanies and empowers the life of a Christian, enabling him to be spiritually effective in his impact and influence on those around him.

The anointing is a result of the working of the Holy Spirit. It is fully supernatural in its origin and effects. At its essence, it is divine power for service.

> The anointing of the Spirit results in power from on high. The person who is anointed will experience a plus factor as he or she works for the kingdom. This edge is necessary to do the work of God effectively (Forbes 1989, 50).

43

The anointing works both in and through the Christian. E. M. Bounds recognized the anointing as a divine influence that comes to the believer through time in prayer. When present, the anointing becomes

> ...the [believer's] entire potential. It inspires and clarifies his intellect, gives insight, grasp, and projecting power. It gives [him] heart power, which is greater than head power. And tenderness, purity, and force flow from the heart by it. Growth, freedom, fullness of thought, directness, and simplicity of utterance are the fruits of this anointing (Bounds 1997, 505).

The anointing also activates and impresses the truth of God on those who hear it. It is the

> sweetest exhalation of the Holy Spirit. It impregnates, suffuses, softens, percolates, cuts, and soothes. It carries the Word like dynamite. It makes the Word a soother, an arraigner, a revealer, a searcher. It makes the hearer a culprit or a saint, makes him weep like a child and live like a giant. It opens his heart and his purse as gently, yet as strongly, as the spring opens the leaves (Bounds 1997, 506).

Dr. Martyn Lloyd-Jones prayerfully sought the anointing throughout his productive preaching ministry in the second half of the twentieth century. As a student of revival, Jones recognized the anointing as the breath of God—a divine impartation of knowledge and power.

> The anointing is the Holy Spirit falling upon the [Christian] in a special manner. It is an access

44

of power. It is God giving power, and enabling, through the Spirit, to [the believer] in order that he may do his work in a manner that lifts up beyond the efforts and endeavors of man to a position in which [he] is being used by the Spirit and becomes the channel through whom the Spirit works (Lloyd-Jones 1976, 305).

The anointing of the Spirit will provide you with power that is divine in origin and transcends human ability. It will enable you to do what you could not naturally accomplish. In a special sense, the anointed believer is in a "zone" that is supernaturally produced by God. This power will bring clarity and understanding to whatever circumstance you are in. It will influence both you and those around you. Often, you will become conscious that a divine power is at work, and this sense of empowerment or "unction" will generate holy boldness. Such boldness is a hallmark of Spirit-anointed speech in the Bible (Micah 3:8; Acts 4:31). Under the anointing, you will experience a clarity of thought and speech, and a heightened sense of authority and confidence. C. H. Spurgeon identified this: "The sacred Spirit can multiply our mental states and make us many times the men we are by nature" (1954, 192).

The impact of an anointed life is unmistakable. A sense of the presence of God can follow a believer's simplest words or actions, bringing conviction of sin and kindling faith in those around him. The anointed Word can bring an awesome awareness of a divine "happening" within the hearts of other Christians. God is there! Under the anointing of the Spirit, the

Scriptures seem suddenly to apply to every twist and turn of life. The impact is holistic; it touches mind, heart, soul, and even the body. You may personally experience renewed energy and strength as a product of your obedience.

Although the anointing has a discernible impact upon people, it is thoroughly a sovereign activity of God's Spirit. The Spirit, like the wind, anoints and blesses as He chooses (John 3:8). His wisdom and timing are of utmost importance. We must desire and prepare for the anointing, but the presence of the anointing and the degree of its power are up to the Lord.

As an activity of God, the anointing is not a permanent possession. There is an ebb and flow of CHARISMA AND divine power in every Christian's life. EARNESTNESS Consequently, you should never take ARE NOT THE the anointing for granted. A feeble ANOINTING. prayer life and careless, carnal living can grieve the Spirit and dissipate the anointing. Take special cautions to remain humble and close to the Lord. Don't hinder the Spirit's work through you, and don't end up like Samson, who, through his carelessness, lost the anointing of God and didn't know it until it was too late (Judges 16:20).

THE ANOINTING AND EMOTIONALISM

People often mistake earnestness, enthusiasm, and personal charisma for the Spirit's anointing. The Spirit will produce earnestness and passion in a person, but an ardent heart is not the same thing as the anointing. Human persuasion in itself is not enough. The supernatural touch is what is needed. The anointing is a divine phenomenon, working in and through the Word of God.

> Anointing is that indefinable, indescribable something that an old, renowned Scottish preacher explained in this manner: "There is sometimes something in preaching that cannot be described either in matter or expression, and cannot be described what it is, or from where it comes, but with a sweet violence it pierces into the heart and affections and comes immediately from the Lord; but if there is any way to obtain such a thing it is by the heavenly disposition of the speaker." We call it unction, or anointing. It is this anointing that makes the Word of God *"quick, and powerful, and sharper than any two-edged sword, piercing even to the dividing asunder of soul and spirit, and of the joints and marrow, and...a discerner of the thoughts and intents of the heart"* (Hebrews 4:12). It is this anointing that gives the words of the preacher such point, sharpness, and power, and that creates such friction and stir in many a dead congregation (Bounds, 504–505).

Sometimes in the African-American church, the anointing is confused with spirited emotionalism. The black preaching and worship traditions are known for their strong, affective tone. The congregation is expected to stomp and shout, and an old adage dictates that the preacher should:

> Start slow,
> rise high,

strike fire,
and sit down in a storm (LaRue 2000, 11).

But the anointing is more than emotive rhetoric. Mere emotionalism doesn't produce divine results. The Holy Spirit's anointing has little to do with cultural style or emotions. It is not a "Pentecostal thing" or a "black thing"; it is a God thing! The true anointing of God can be recognized only by divine results and enduring spiritual fruit.

Back in the beginning of the Great Awakening in New England, the Puritan pastor and theologian Jonathan Edwards read his sermon, *Sinners in the Hands of an Angry God,* from a handwritten manuscript. His delivery was undramatic and unaffected. Edwards' eyesight was bad, and he had to keep the manuscript close to his eyes. In spite of these encumbrances, the anointing was powerful on his ministry. The congregation felt the wrath of God revealed so vividly that grown men clung to the pillars to keep from falling into the smoking abyss of hell. The impact of Edwards' ministry—like those of so many of God's giants—was not manipulation, but a genuine display of the anointed life.

The Spirit's anointing is real. It isn't a result of emotional manipulation or mass psychology. The anointing is a demonstration of spiritual reality. It can't be faked or mimicked. The anointing is a reflection of what goes on behind the scenes; it demonstrates God's willingness to bless His children and the intense prayer, submission, and spiritual preparation of a Christian's heart. What is revealed daily is the alignment of the believer's heart and spirit with the sovereign purposes of the Lord.

QUESTIONS FOR REFLECTION AND DISCUSSION

1. Describe a time when you deeply realized your utter dependency on God.

2. How close is your personal relationship with the Spirit of the Lord? What do you do to cultivate this relationship? What do you do that quenches or frustrates the Spirit?

3. How do you experience the Spirit's help and direction in your place of work?

4. Provide a personal definition for the anointing. Upon what biblical and theological supports do you base your definition?

5. What has been the anointing's influence upon you? How has it impacted those within your sphere of influence?

6. How would you distinguish between the influence of mere emotionalism and the genuine work of the Spirit's anointing?

CHAPTER THREE

GOD'S POWER AND LIGHT COMPANY

GOD'S POWER AND LIGHT COMPANY

The power that is in the Gospel does not lie in the eloquence of the [believer]; otherwise men would be converters of souls. Nor does it lie in the [Christian's] learning; otherwise it would consist in the wisdom of men. We might [talk] till our tongues rotted, till we should exhaust our lungs and die, but never a soul would be converted unless there were mysterious power going with it—the Holy Spirit changing the will of man. O sirs! We might as well preach to stone walls as preach to humanity unless the Holy Spirit is with the word, to give power to convert the soul.
—C. H. Spurgeon

God's heart is crying for a renaissance of spirit-led life among His people. It's not by His choice that we fumble through life, far from the power and intimacy of the New Testament church. Rather, it is His plan to empower us with the anointing. **Remember, the anointing is a special, sovereign activity of the Holy Spirit that accompanies and empowers the life of a Christian, enabling him to be spiritually effective in his impact and influence on those around him.**

The question is, how does the anointing work? We need truths that do more than resonate nicely off hardwood pews. What is there in this anointed life that we can take with us every day?

The Spirit-led life stands on two "legs." I call them "the transforming Word" and "prophecy and power." These legs are the two main ways in which the Holy Spirit anoints believers. Unfortunately, few Christians ever learn a balanced view of the Spirit's ministry. The Pentecostal and Charismatic traditions isolate His role as power—divine energy for special occasions. The Evangelical tradition focuses upon His role as light—bringing the Word to life; encouraging and convicting (Foster 1998; 8–9, 14–18). It's no wonder that the church isn't as effective as we should be—most of the time, we're running the race while hopping on one leg! The even sadder truth is that some Christians spend their whole lives without paying any attention to the Spirit of the Lord at all.

I try not to be dogmatic about the details. Traditional Baptist theology doesn't have a systematic understanding of the anointing, and, although I am Baptist, I am often asked if I am a Pentecostal. So I understand that the phrase *filled with the Spirit* can be very confusing. Most of the problem is a matter of wording—using the same words to describe different sides of the Spirit's work.

Sometimes Scripture uses *filled with the Spirit* to refer to a process of sanctification (being transformed by the Word, from the inside out). Other times, it uses exactly the same words to talk about the supernatural abilities that are given to Christians for specific occasions.

THE TRANSFORMING WORD

As I understand it, the Holy Spirit enters a person when he accepts Jesus Christ as Lord and Savior. The apostle Paul recognized the new-creation experience as a fundamental reality of Christian life (Fee 1994, 330–332). This concept of "newness" was one of his favorites. He said in Romans 8:5–11 that, by definition, a Christian is someone who has the Holy Spirit living in his heart and working to change his sinful nature. Once you accept Christ, you must purposely allow the Spirit to change your heart and help you to live in a way that is pleasing to God. This is a deepening relationship with the Spirit of God, and it will naturally produce the fruits of a Christlike life.

THE HOLY SPIRIT WORKS IN YOU TO CHANGE YOUR NATURE.

In this sense, being filled with the Spirit is just surrendering total control of your life to God. It's the transforming Word at work. Paul described this in Romans 6, comparing it to the way Jesus surrendered His life on the cross. But our surrender has to take place every day, as we learn to let go, piece by piece.

It might be helpful to use the gas furnace in a home as an analogy. That furnace has a pilot light. If the pilot light is out, the furnace is incapable of producing heat. The light must be lit. When a person is saved, the pilot light of his spirit is lit by the Holy Spirit. There is now some light and heat, but the house is still mostly cold. Imagine trying to heat your home by the pilot light alone! The thermostat has to be set and the furnace kicked on. Then, slowly, the warm air fills the whole structure. This is a process of permeation. The potential for heat is there as soon as the pilot light comes on—but the furnace will work only if the thermostat allows it to.

In the same way, every Christian has the Holy Spirit living inside him. Potentially, He can bring the presence and reality of Jesus into each life. You can choose to settle for little more than the pilot light, or you can have the mighty power of the whole roaring furnace filling your life. Then you will truly be transformed into a new creation.

Submitting to the transforming Word isn't very glamorous, and it doesn't preach very well. Nobody really wants to hear about God rearranging their mental furniture. But it is the only foundation for an anointed life.

Paul wrote 2 Corinthians to deal with a leadership crisis in the Corinthian church. A steady stream of supposed super-apostles were goose-stepping through the pulpit there. They came with fancy letters of recommendation and took every opportunity to sling mud at Paul. They insulted the way he talked, and they criticized his apparent lack of pedigree. In his letter, Paul didn't take on these accusations head-to-head. Instead, he pointed with powerful assurance to the transforming Word that worked in and through him. In his own words, *"But he that glorieth, let him glory in the Lord. For not he that commendeth himself is approved, but whom the Lord commendeth"* (2 Corinthians 10:17–18).

A scientist who studied birds once revealed the secret as to why storks and herons stand on one leg for long periods of time: If they pick up the other leg, they fall down.

He was joking, but I'm very serious. As I said before, it is a sad thing when Christians cannot walk on both legs of the anointed life. But this transforming work of the Spirit is the leg upon which we will stand or fall. We need prophecy and power to run the race, but, without submission to Christ's nature, we are guaranteed to fall.

PROPHECY AND POWER

Since the Old Testament, God has anointed His chosen people with supernatural abilities, as the need arose. Second Kings chapter three tells how a three-nation alliance, including God's people, was cornered in a desert valley by the superbly organized Moabite army. In desperation, the kings of Israel and Judah called for the prophet Elisha and asked him to seek God on their behalf. God told Elisha, *"Make this valley full of ditches. For thus saith the LORD, Ye shall not see wind, neither shall ye see rain; yet that valley shall be filled with water, that ye may drink, both ye, and your cattle, and your beasts"* (2 Kings 3:16–17).

Strange as it seemed, they dug the ditches, which slowly filled with water during the night. (The Bible isn't clear whether God had them tap into an underground spring, or if He simply created the water on the spot.) The next morning, Moabite lookouts saw the red sunrise glinting off the water, lying (or so they thought) all over the ground. Mistaking it for blood, they concluded that they were seeing the result of a fallout between the members of the Israelite alliance! Abandoning all military discipline, the whole Moabite army scrambled down the hillsides and into the camp, where God's army was grimly waiting in ambush.

Thanks to the supernatural gifting of Elisha, God's people were saved from being killed in a corner. Instead, they smashed the core of Moab's army and then demolished the pagans' outposts. In a short time, they had pushed the Moabites back deep into their own country.

Long after that, God gifted a young man named Samson with inhuman strength. As a freedom fighter, Samson took on whole armies single-handedly and won—sometimes without a proper weapon! And long, long before that, God had given Joseph the ability to interpret dreams. He used this gift to place Joseph, a

ARE YOU OPEN TO DISCERNING AND DOING GOD'S WILL? righteous man of wisdom, in a position to save Egypt from a terrible famine. From age to age, all the way through the Old Testament, God always had at least one servant with a special ability to discern His will or execute His plan. In fact, God's heart on the matter was probably summed up perfectly by Moses, in Numbers 11. Let's look at that story now.

Governing the people of Israel had gotten to be too large a task for one man. God told Moses to select seventy well-respected elders as governors. They held a ceremony of prayer, dedicating these men and asking God to pour onto them the same anointing that was on Moses.

To everyone's amazement, all the elders simultaneously began to prophesy (including two who had been unable to make the ceremony and were partway across town)! Joshua, Moses' young protégé, protested against what he saw as an infringement on Moses' office. But Moses shushed him. *"Are you jealous for my sake? Would that all the LORD's people were prophets, that the LORD would put His Spirit upon them!"* (Numbers 11:29 NASB).

The prophecy-and-power "leg" seems to have faded out during the years that passed between the Old and New Testament records. It seems that God sent no prophets until John the Baptist began to herald Jesus' arrival as Messiah. Scripture records that John was filled with a special power while he was still in his mother's womb (Luke 1:15), and his preaching carried an authority that baffled his enemies.

As God incarnate, Jesus was the consummate example of an anointed servant. He fulfilled the prophetic legacy of Isaiah 61:

> *The spirit of the Lord GOD is upon me; because the LORD hath anointed me to preach good tidings unto the meek; he hath sent me to bind up the brokenhearted, to proclaim liberty to the captives, and the opening of the prison to them that*

*are bound; to proclaim the acceptable year of the
Lord, and the day of vengeance of our God; to
comfort all that mourn; to appoint unto them
that mourn in Zion, to give unto them beauty for
ashes, the oil of joy for mourning, the garment of
praise for the spirit of heaviness; that they might
be called trees of righteousness, the planting of
the Lord, that he might be glorified.* (vv. 1–3)

Before He ascended into heaven, Jesus promised His
disciples that He would send them power from on
high—anointing them to become a witness to all nations
(Luke 24:48–49). The book of Acts tells how this promise
was fulfilled, and—according to Moses' desire—all the
believers were filled with the Spirit. They spoke with
power, performed miracles, made decisions based on
divine revelation, and turned the Roman world upside
down. (See Acts 4:8; 13:9.)

But What about Now?

That was my question, soon after I was saved. "What
about now? What about me?" Just before I left home
for college, I started attending my cousin's church. He
was a Pentecostal preacher. I was raised in a Baptist
church, and, as I was a new believer, the teaching about
gifts of the Spirit got my attention. One Sunday eve-
ning, after the sermon, my cousin gave a general invitation to anyone who wanted to be filled with the Holy
Spirit. I went forward to the prayer altar. As I knelt in
prayer, several people surrounded me and began praying for me. While they prayed with me, they encour-
aged me to speak in other tongues. I was tense and a

little scared, and I resented how much they were coaxing me. I finished praying and went back to my pew. While I was sitting there, something amazing happened to me. I can say only that I suddenly felt like I was transported into another realm—a reality nearer to God. This lasted for a few minutes, and when I came back to my normal senses, several people around me told me that I was speaking in an unknown language.

This frightened me a bit, and for several years I kept the Spirit at arm's length. For the first part of my pastoral ministry, I stayed away from the supernatural reality that I had tasted. As a young Baptist pastor, I was striving to stay in line with the theological and cultural boundaries of my denomination. The Spirit would occasionally "annoy" me about resisting Him, but I felt boxed in by a lot of factors. In fact, it took a crisis in my life to crack me open to the Spirit's work in my life. Since then, I have developed a growing hunger and appreciation for the unique operations of God's Spirit.

SPIRITUAL GIFTS STILL WORK AS THEY DID IN THE EARLY CHURCH.

Now our beliefs and practices at Salem Church (my congregation) resemble traditional Pentecostal doctrine, though they aren't identical. We believe that God gives believers transforming, supernatural experiences, in which they receive His power for specific tasks or problems. The gifts of the Spirit function today as surely as they did in the New Testament church. There is no good scriptural case for arguing that they should have ceased, and I have both seen and experienced the gifts of healing, knowledge, prophecy, wisdom, discernment, and tongues. These are individual experiences that come at specific times for specific tasks or services. So a believer can be filled again and again with prophecy and power.

The gifts of the Spirit are given at the discretion of the Holy Spirit alone. I believe that every Christian is given the potential for his own tailored set of spiritual gifts when he accepts Jesus Christ as Lord and Savior. As he grows, it is his responsibility to let the transforming Word work in his heart, and to ask God to use him in an "ordinary" day-to-day fashion. The gifts will then come naturally, because God designed them primarily to build up His church and give authority to the Gospel (2 Corinthians 10:8).

Don't think I take these things lightly. These are not "superpowers" or magic rings. Every time a believer uses a spiritual gift, God Himself, motivated by His incredible love, is interrupting the natural order of the universe.

Analysis of the Anointed Life

What all this means is that there are four things that characterize the anointed life. No matter how personal the Spirit's work, these things are always true.

Anointed Life Is God-Dependent

The apostle Paul was personally convinced that his new-covenant life came from God, was for God, and was accomplished through God. Paul recognized that only the power of the Spirit could make his life meaningful.

So Paul relied completely on the Spirit to do His life-giving work (2 Corinthians 3:6). If God did not call and anoint him (2 Corinthians 1:21–22), Paul had no hope of being a success. He was adequate only through God's grace—and he liked it that way! This God-dependent living made him impossible to manipulate, and it kept him from the temptation to act more spiritual than he was. (Go back to 2 Corinthians and read the outrage in his voice if you don't believe me!) Paul tried with all his heart to speak the truth clearly, relying on the Spirit of God to drive it home to those who heard him (2 Corinthians 4:2).

ANOINTED LIFE IS CHRIST-CENTERED

Paul preached Jesus Christ as Lord (v. 5). More important, Paul lived as though Jesus Christ was his Lord. His daily goal was to bring honor to Christ (v. 4). It was His death on the cross that reconciled humanity to God, inaugurated the new covenant, and provided the gift of His righteousness to all who believe (2 Corinthians 5:18, 21). Without Jesus, our faith is a hollow eggshell of busywork. Jesus wasn't just the content of Paul's preaching—He was the center of his life.

ANOINTED LIVING REFLECTS THE TRANSFORMING WORD

The essence of new-covenant life is the transformation of human hearts (2 Corinthians 3:2–3; 3:18). New-covenant living is possible only through the life-giving and illuminating power of the Holy Spirit (v. 6). You are called to be an agent of revelation because you, through the Gospel, have seen the light! This light reveals the glory of God in the life of Christ. As a steward of this life, you share the light of God through your words and actions.

The supernatural process of salvation and transformation is governed by the Spirit of the Lord. Only God can bring about these changes. Therefore, even in your weakness and inadequacy, God can use you to reach people with His love! In fact, God delights to use the weakness of Christians and their lives in order to show that the power at work is truly His. You are simply a clay vessel used for God's glory (2 Corinthians 4:7).

The transforming Word "leg" has had an incredible impact upon my life and ministry. While the prophecy- and-power anointing awakens sinners and builds faith in my congregation, it is the steady work of the Spirit that saves and transforms me and my flock. My most powerful ministry is the one all Christians share: God works through me to reveal Jesus. This can come only through the anointing of the Spirit, and this is why I daily seek through humble prayer the anointing of God's Spirit.

GOD CAN USE YOU, NO MATTER HOW WEAK YOU MAY FEEL.

Anointed Life Is Spirit-Empowered

Many of the greatest preachers and revivalists have depended on the anointing of prophecy and power. Let's look at how the following men were empowered by the Holy Spirit in their ministry.

Charles Finney

Finney, the great American evangelist, was dramatically endowed with the Spirit's power early in life.

> I could feel the impression, like a wave of electricity, going through me. Indeed, it seemed to come

in waves of liquid love....These waves came over me and over me, one after the other, until I cried out, "I will die if these waves continue to pass over me!" I said, "Lord, I cannot bear any more" (Finney 1999, 24–25).

Finney's baptism in the Holy Spirit had a lasting impact on his preaching ministry. He firmly believed this gift was given to "savingly impress men," and it's true that a powerful anointing often evidenced itself through his preaching. He said,

I immediately found myself clothed with such power from on high that a few words dropped here and there to individuals were the means of their immediate conversion. My words seemed to fasten like barbed arrows in the souls of men. They cut like a sword. They broke the heart like a hammer. Multitudes can attest to this....This power seems sometimes to pervade the atmosphere of one who is highly charged with it (2000; 20, 22).

George Whitefield

A renowned revivalist of the Great Awakening, Whitefield experienced the anointing of God's power at his ordination service. He knew it, and he was thrilled with the sense of divine ability it brought. His very first sermon was in his hometown of Gloucester, and it shook the community (Lloyd-Jones 1972, 320)! Whitefield often referred to the "thunder and lightning" in his sermons. By this he meant that he felt the power of God come upon him, equipping him with an unusual authority and dynamism (Lloyd-Jones 1987, 122).

Dwight Moody

Moody candidly recorded the day when, on Wall Street in New York City, he was visited from on high. The power of God fell on Moody as he walked down the street, and he was so overwhelmed that he hurried to a friend and asked for a room for the day. While he was there, the Spirit filled him with so much joy that he begged God to stop. Moody said later:

> I was crying all the time that God would anoint me with His Spirit. Well, one day, in the city of New York—oh, what a day!—I cannot describe it....I can only say that God revealed Himself to me, and I had such an experience of His love that I had to ask Him to stay His hand. I went to preaching again. The sermons were not different; I did not present any new truths; yet hundreds were converted. I would not now be placed back to where I was before that blessed experience if you would give me all the world (Choy 1990, 121).

As a result of this anointing, Moody's ministry took on a supernatural impact. He admitted that, after this encounter with the Spirit, he preached the same messages as he had before, and with the same style of delivery. The difference was in the results of his preaching! Tens of thousands were ushered into the kingdom as a result of his anointed preaching.

You!

Christian, what about you? God wants you to live in the power and life-giving anointing of the Holy Spirit. The life of the new covenant is one of the Spirit. Only the Spirit can reveal, liberate, and transform you into the likeness of Christ. God wants to fill you with His Spirit and anoint your life. What was available to the great preachers of the past is available to you!

Whenever I start a day, I ask for anointing from the Lord. I seek the empowerment from the Lord I need in order to act and speak in a way that will truly honor God and accomplish His purposes. I ask to be used beyond human ability through the influence of the Holy Spirit—even if that just means being patient and loving with someone who isn't very patient or loving toward me.

One thing you absolutely must remember is to stay open to the Spirit. Although you might not be comfortable thinking of yourself as a messenger, the Spirit may want to use you in a unique but powerful **GOD WANTS TO FILL YOU WITH HIS SPIRIT.** manner. Please don't put God in a box. Be open, and you will be surprised at what the Lord will do through you. You may also be surprised at how much you like it!

This is one thing that continues to make life such an adventure for me. When my feet hit the floor each morning, I'm never sure what God may be up to. All I know is that I want to be a part of it!

QUESTIONS FOR REFLECTION AND DISCUSSION

1. What "leg" of the Holy Spirit do you find yourself most involved in? In what ways does this demonstrate itself in your life and ministry? What could you do to develop a greater awareness of the other "leg" in your life?

2. What does the filling of the Spirit mean to you? Have you experienced it in your life? Describe briefly a time when you felt "filled with the Spirit" to minister for God.

3. What spiritual gifts do you regularly exercise? How do these gifts play a role in your witness of God's Word?

4. What does it mean to prophesy? Have you ever experienced a time when you felt God gave you words to speak? Write a short paragraph describing it.

5. What role does your understanding of new-creation realities play in your own Christian life and experience? How do they impact your study of God's Word in terms of producing revelation, liberation, and transformation?

CHAPTER FOUR

THE CALL

CHAPTER FOUR

THE CALL

To truly understand the anointing, you must understand its purpose. To understand the purpose of the anointing, you must understand the calling of God, because the two are linked. You probably remember that anointing with oil was an Old Testament symbol of God's calling on a person's life. It's very important that we also remember that the calling always came before the anointing. David was chosen by God as king of Israel long before Samuel ever arrived to anoint him. Before Jesus was filled with the anointing of power, the Father spoke from heaven, *"This is my beloved Son, in whom I am well pleased"* (Matthew 3:17).

In fact, God's calling is the foundation for the anointing. See, God's call on your life is about who He wants you to become, and not necessarily about what He wants you to do. The "legs" of the anointing are your strength for the journey. The transforming Word "leg" will shape your character, making you a person of integrity. The prophecy-and-power "leg" will give you the abilities you need.

The anointing is about identity, because God's desire is for you to be *"conformed to the image of his Son"* (Romans 8:29). That is something that none of us can do—an identity none of us can ever gain in our own strength. The anointing is there because we cannot answer the call ourselves. In a manner of speaking, it's traditional—God always calls people who are hopelessly under-equipped. Think about it: God wanted a messenger to stand up to Egypt's Pharaoh and demand *"Let my people go"* (Exodus 5:1). So he picked Moses, who was terrified of public speaking! (See Exodus 4:10–12.) When God wanted a warrior to free His people from the tyranny of the Midianites, He hunted up Gideon—who was hiding like a scared rabbit!

And now we're living in the age when God has called all believers into the service of the kingdom, as the apostle Peter said,

> *This is that which was spoken by the prophet Joel;*
> *And it shall come to pass in the last days, saith*
> *God, I will pour out of my Spirit upon all flesh:*
> *and your sons and your daughters shall prophesy,*
> *and your young men shall see visions, and your*
> *old men shall dream dreams: and on my servants*
> *and on my handmaidens I will pour out in those*
> *days of my Spirit.* (Acts 2:16–18)

Romans 12 lists a host of spiritual callings—all the way from preaching and prophesying to encouraging and giving. And Paul commanded, *"Having then gifts differing according to the grace that is given to us...let us* [use them] *according to the proportion of faith"* (v. 6).

You'll note that I paraphrased part of the verse. It would be worth your time to read the whole passage, from verse five to the end of the chapter. Not only did Paul list a staggering number of gifts and callings, but he also explained how the focus of the anointing changes from one to the next. No one is left out—everyone has a call, and an anointing to go with it.

You are called by God to live an anointed life. Great! So how do you know what you're called to?

THE CALL TO SALVATION

This might seem insultingly basic, but the first part of your calling is the call from Calvary. If Christ is not your Lord and Savior, there is no way His Spirit can be at work in you. Sadly, it is possible to be a solid church-goer and a terrific person without being a Christian.

In fact, it's possible to be a minister of the Gospel without ever being a Christian! John Wesley, the revivalist founder of the Methodist Church, did just that for years. He served for many years as an Anglican cleric and missionary, pouring himself out in an effort to please God. But, by his own accounting, his heart and ministry languished until a revelation of the Gospel "strangely warmed" his heart. After his conversion, God used John Wesley to bring thousands to salvation.

THE FIRST PART OF YOUR CALLING IS THE CALL FROM CALVARY.

I had a similar experience. I was raised in church and considered myself a Christian, sort of like I'd absorbed it through my pores. I was even baptized at age twelve, not realizing that I was missing a personal encounter with God's grace. It was some years later when a revivalist pastor ended his sermon with an invitation: "If you really want to know Jesus Christ, please come forward to the altar. If you want Jesus and the Holy Spirit to become a living presence in your life, come forward tonight."

I had never knelt at the altar before—I'd gone to the front of the church when I joined the church, but I'd never come forward to meet with God. But I felt as if someone was tugging me forward. The preacher said I needed God, and I felt my need. I can still see myself at that altar, my neighbor and another lady kneeling beside me and praying with me. I prayed as a needy sinner accepting Christ into my life, and I felt His tender love surround me. I was changed before I stood up—my heart was softer toward God, and wrong habits seemed to lose their grip on me. Even my parents noticed a change in me, and thankfully they took it as confirmation that my life belonged to Christ.

Personal salvation requires that three things be true. First, you must understand the message of the Bible: The human race is fallen, prone to evil, and that evil directs their lives away from God and into hell. God is blindingly perfect, and His divine justice cannot allow sin to go unpunished. But He is also impossibly loving, and He sent His only Son to take the punishment. Because Jesus was perfect, He was able to take the judgment of the entire human race, pay our debt, and rise from the dead, with authority over hell and judgment.

Second, you have to accept the message as truth. Jesus lived, walked, and died in a historical place. The leader of Jerusalem's government had His name on records that we have rediscovered today. The Gospel is more than a legend—it's history!

Finally, you have a choice. You can acknowledge Jesus' sacrifice in sort of the same way that a careless person might acknowledge Lincoln's Emancipation Proclamation—merely as interesting history. Or you can accept His offer of freedom, choosing to live in the freedom that His lordship can bring you. A true Christian is someone who has had a moment of truth—a point at which he looked divine judgment in the face, admitted it was real, and chose to accept God's mercy.

A vibrant, anointed life always grows out of a true salvation experience. Whether you look back at a life of sin or depression and thank God for rescuing you, or you look back at a childhood salvation experience, God's grace should be a source of joy for you. That joy is the power core of the anointed life.

THE INTERNAL CALL

God will move on your heart, leading you toward the calling He wants you to become. (Don't forget—the calling is an identity, and the anointing is His means of shaping you.) It is hard to pin down the internal calling. Because it's personal, it can be subjective. But there is a pattern to how God speaks.

Often, the direction of someone's calling will begin to show itself in a nagging feeling of responsibility. In other words, if your calling is to be a friend to the guy next door (you know, the one with the pickup truck

YOUR CALLING MIGHT ORIGINATE WITH A FEELING OF RESPONSIBILITY. and the "Keep honking—I'm reloading" bumper sticker), you may suddenly find yourself thinking about the state of his soul every time you see his truck. People often take their first stumbling steps into their callings because, all of a sudden, they are confronted with the same need everywhere they go, until they become convinced that somebody should do something about it. Then, one way or another, God whispers, "What about you?"

A young man, currently a biochemist at John Hopkins University and a friend of mine, is making slow, prayerful preparation to become a missionary to India. How on earth does someone get a calling like that? Well, for Matt there was a sermon about missions, where the preacher touched briefly on India. Then, for years after that, everywhere he went, he saw India. We aren't just talking magazines with articles on India—we're talking the shape of India in the pattern of a carpet, or the wood grain of a table, or the cracks in a concrete slab. Matt says it was really strange, but the images were so persistent that he began to pray about them, until he finally felt a peace that God was truly calling him.

Your calling probably won't be to drop your job and head overseas (although, for one or two people reading this, it just might be). But that doesn't make your calling any less of a commitment, and it might even seem to be harder!

Go back to work—only today you need to walk away from the water fountain when Jon starts telling his off-color joke. You might need to use your day off to help someone shingle a roof. Maybe you'll have to be loving toward your husband when he forgets to take his boots off, and tracks mud onto your new carpet.

When it finally dawns, finding your calling is usually a sobering thing. As soon as you answer "Who does God want me to be?" you realize that the much bigger question is, "How am I ever going to be like that?"

The logistical problems might seem huge: Your neighbor hunts big game for a living. You work for an ad agency. He's fiercely liberal (on everything but gun control); you're pretty conservative. He's a fan of the World Wrestling Federation. You prefer miniature golf. Oh, and he has that V-8 pickup with off-road suspension and trailer gearing. You drive a Volvo station wagon.

Why would he ever want to talk to you? Why should you talk to him? What on earth do you have in common?

The point is, no matter what your calling is, you can't do it yourself—that's what the anointing is for. But, typically, believers struggle at this point. They feel insecure, or maybe even resent God's efforts to change them. We love to upgrade everything—until it gets to character development. Then, suddenly, we're growling the old-fashioned wisdom, "If it ain't broke, don't fix it."

Acknowledging the internal call climaxes in a moment of submission to God's will. Let me encourage you—just do it! I know that Nike has that phrase trade-marked, but indulge me for a moment. God offers you His unconditional love, supernatural peace and joy, and spiritual power of biblical proportions. He wants you to give Him your life completely, so that He can make it a story worth envying. (See Matthew 19:28–30.) Is that too much to ask?

SCRIPTURAL CONFIRMATION

Do you want a checkpoint against which you can evaluate your internal calling, just to make sure you're not getting carried away? Good. That's exactly what the Bible is for. In fact, God laid out clear requirements for certain kinds of ministry. Let's say, for example, that you were interested in becoming an elder or some other kind of governor in your church. First Timothy has very clear guidelines about who should serve in that capacity, and who should not. For instance, look at verses four and five of 1 Timothy 3:

> *One that ruleth well his own house, having his children in subjection with all gravity; (for if a man know not how to rule his own house, how shall he take care of the church of God?)*

Now, suppose that your children have a tendency to come when they're called—the fifth time—and are just generally difficult to control. You're probably on your way to being a good parent, but you haven't been one yet! Give yourself time to learn how to govern your house in a Christlike spirit before you try to govern in God's house. Chances are, if you patiently learn that, He will lead you right to a place of leadership.

Also, Paul said that new believers shouldn't be given too much authority (v. 6). It's to protect them against pride—one of the most subtle, and most deadly, of the enemy's traps. Don't give up hope, and don't think that your calling was false. If God is making you a leader, why don't you see about gathering a group of men to help rewire old Sister Margaret's kitchen? Or if you feel a call to represent Christ's love, why don't you volunteer as an usher at your church? Every service, you'll see dozens of faces that need the light of His love and acceptance.

As Paul said in Romans 15:2, we're all called to edify (encourage and build up) each other. There is no shame in the "lesser" tasks. Jesus said that, as far as He was concerned, the way we treat the "little people" is the way we treat Him (Matthew 25:40). Besides, between greeting people at the door and organizing that work day, you might discover that you have a spiritual gift for helps or administration. It could change your whole approach to anointed living! Stranger things have happened.

THE WAY WE TREAT THE "LITTLE PEOPLE" IS HOW WE TREAT JESUS.

WHAT ARE YOUR GIFTS?

If you're trying to understand your calling, take a look at the gifts God has given you. They can be a good indicator, because your spiritual gifts and talents are already tailored to your calling. Nobody plans ahead like God does. So if you have strong teaching or prophetic gifts but are rather disorganized in your personal life (you know who you are), you probably aren't called to anything that will require an administrative or organizational gift. But it might mean that you should pray more seriously about volunteering for that empty spot as a Sunday school teacher.

That said, your gifts are only an indicator of the nature of your calling. Sometimes they're a good indicator, but you can't use them as a solid principle. Most people have undiscovered spiritual gifts in the frontier of their souls. It's entirely possible that God could call you to an administrative task. If He does, the gift will be there when you arrive.

CONFIRMATION OF THE COMMUNITY OF FAITH

In the Old Testament, God called a lot of lone rangers. Samson fought alone. Jeremiah faced a whole community of false prophets with only God behind him. There was a large remnant of believers in Elijah's time, but he stood by himself to confront the wicked Baal worshippers. But things changed in the New Testament. God is no longer satisfied with a community of believers that produce a maverick prophet here and there. He desires to have a community of faith—a community of believers who all walk in the love and power of the anointing.

The apostle Paul had one of the most dramatic conversions anyone has ever had. He was riding a horse, on the way to arrest and kill Christians, because he believed that they were heretics. God physically (though invisibly) knocked Paul off his horse, blinded him, and spoke audibly to him.

After that, you'd think he was ready to start a revolution! But God told him to go to a certain house and wait.

After a while, God sent a mature Christian to pray with Paul and guide him into his calling. Through another believer, Paul was given a confirmation of God's call upon his life.

In 1 Timothy 4:14, Paul made it clear that Timothy was sent to his work with the prayers and blessing of the faith community. Acts 6:1–6 tells how the believers chose seven men to organize the charitable care of widow and orphans, and the apostles laid hands on them in prayer, blessing their new calling.

COUNT THE COST

When you feel God's calling, make sure you include responsible Christians in your decision. Talk to your wife before you try to strike up a conversation with the outdoorsman across the street. Ask her to pray that God will help you find common ground with him. Humbly submit your application for the position as an usher. Accept instruction, and be ready to do the jobs that no one will see.

When you do find your calling, you must embrace the identity God has created for you. It's not a day job, and it's not a hobby. The foundation for the anointed life is a heart that is completely sold out to God's will.

> Calling is the truth that God calls us to Himself so decisively that everything we are, everything we do, and everything we have is invested with a special devotion and dynamism lived out as a response to His summons and service (Guinness 1998, 4).

This isn't something to do lightly—that's why the accountability of the faith community is so important.

YOU MIGHT NEED TO SACRIFICE FOR YOUR CALLING. Jesus urged, *"Whosoever will come after me, let him deny himself, and take up his cross, and follow me"* (Mark 8:34). Don't run headlong into your calling unless you're prepared to sacrifice for it. Otherwise, the first difficulty might swat you out of the air like a limp shuttlecock. *"And Jesus said unto him, No man, having put his hand to the plow, and looking back, is fit for the kingdom of God"* (Luke 9:62).

Count the cost, but remember what Jesus promised: *"For...whosoever shall lose his life for my sake and the gospel's, the same shall save it"* (Mark 8:35).

QUESTIONS FOR REFLECTION AND DISCUSSION

1. When did you first realize that God has a special purpose for your life? How did that affect where you are today?

2. When you first recognized God was calling you, did you have initial fears about accepting His call? What were they? How did God confirm His plan for your life?

3. How has your sense of calling changed over time? What do you do to remind yourself of God's purpose for you?

4. What price have you paid to follow God's call? What does it mean for you to take up your cross and follow Jesus every day?

5. If you haven't yet felt the call of God upon your life, what things could you do to discover it?

CHAPTER FIVE

BECOMING

BECOMING

*The world has not yet seen what God can do through a man
who is totally yielded to God.*
—D. L. Moody

*"Sometimes," said the Skin Horse, for he was always
truthful. "When you are real, you don't mind being hurt."
"Does it happen all at once, like being wound up," he [the
Velveteen Rabbit] asked, "or bit by bit?"
"It doesn't happen all at once," said the Skin Horse. "You
become. It takes a long time. That's why it doesn't happen to
people who break easily, or have sharp edges, or who have
to be carefully kept. Generally, by the time you are real,
most of your hair has rubbed off, and your eyes drop out
and you get loose in the joints and very shabby. But these
don't matter at all, because when you are real you can't be
ugly, except to people who don't understand.*
—Margery Williams Bianco, *The Velveteen Rabbit*

Surrender

We talked in the last chapter about how the calling is an identity, not just a job. God values authenticity above all else. For Him, being real is the name of the game, and nobody could explain why better than Jesus did:

> *Do men gather grapes of thorns, or figs of thistles? Even so every good tree bringeth forth good fruit; but a corrupt tree bringeth forth evil fruit. A good tree cannot bring forth evil fruit, neither can a corrupt tree bring forth good fruit. Every tree that bringeth not forth good fruit is hewn down, and cast into the fire. Wherefore by their fruits ye shall know them.* (Matthew 7:16–20)

Benjamin Disraeli, a prime minister of England in the 1800s, once gave a powerful address to the House of Parliament. Afterward, an admirer asked him how long he'd spent preparing for that thirty-minute speech.

"Twenty years," he replied soberly before moving on.

Every word we say and every action we perform comes through the filter of who we are inside. If you don't allow the anointing to change you—if you try to live for God without really making Him your Lord—you will fail. Without the Holy Spirit working in your life, you're a thistle bush at heart, and you'll never produce the fruits of the Spirit.

On the other hand, if you completely surrender to Him, you will open the door to His supernatural activity in your life. The apostle Paul demonstrated this truth in his own life. He was the model of an authentic Christian. Paul considered himself a servant of Jesus and the church (2 Corinthians 4:5). He tried not to manipulate his public image, he avoided promoting himself whenever he could, and he was always sincere. What you saw in Paul was what you got from him—rough edges and in-your-face preaching included. He even made himself vulnerable to the people around him, being completely honest about his struggles and weaknesses (2 Corinthians 2:2–5).

The result? God used Paul to start dozens of churches, raise people from the dead, and lead hundreds of people to Christ. Most important, even unsaved people respected Paul—despite his unbelievable conversion story and dogged proselytizing—because of the integrity and openness of his life (Acts 26).

MUD WRESTLING WITH GOD

The journey to anointed power climbs a hilly path of increasing brokenness and surrender to God. The love of God is pretty stubborn, and I don't think He ever gives up trying to mold us into something He can bless and use. Because the anointing is His power to do what we cannot, we have to recognize that we are weak. That's all spiritual brokenness is. For some people, it comes very easily—that's the childlike heart that God loves. But most people (can we blame part of it on our go-getter society?) refuse to admit that there's anything they can't do. Too often, God is forced to take us through one difficult

THE ANOINTED LIFE REQUIRES BROKENNESS AND SURRENDER.

circumstance after another, until we finally fall to our knees under the weight of life. Then, humbled at last, we're in a position to ask Him to do what He's always wanted to do—carry the burden for us.

Calvin Miller said it very well:

> God's power comes only as the prize of spiritual submission.…There are very few [believers] who are willing to be a channel of any power that does not originate in themselves. The buzzword for this is surrender. Surrender rightly implies a relinquishment of all that might be in God's way that prevents the [Christian] from becoming a channel (1996, 65).

I'm pretty well qualified to talk about this subject, because complete surrender has been my lifelong struggle. The flesh dies hard, but God keeps refusing to let me hide from His grace. In fact, He pokes into the areas of my greatest fears and insecurities, drags them (usually kicking and screaming) into the light, and then mercifully heals them.

There is a lot of Jacob's nature in me. If you'll remember from Genesis, Jacob was not really wicked so much as he used his own skills to maintain control. He didn't really surrender to God until one night well into his adult life. God appeared to him in the form of a man, on the bank of the river Jabbok. They wrestled there, in the mud—classical wrestling, with moves that took hours to complete and strained sinews to their limit. Finally, God touched Jacob's thigh and supernaturally popped it out of joint. Jacob walked with a limp for the rest of his life. It was God's reminder that, no matter how successful Jacob would become, God was the One in charge. (See Genesis 32:22–32.) And then God blessed him.

Like Jacob, I strive to keep control—especially in those areas of my life that generate a deep sense of fear and inadequacy. I struggled against God's call for my life because I was afraid of being changed from a pretty fly Jinwright into a pastor-guy. Once I accepted that God wasn't going to make me a "normal" person, I wanted to be in charge of the ministry He gave me. After all, I was a businessman at heart—until God changed that, too.

These were my Jabboks, those places where I found myself wrestling with God in the mud. At each pivotal point in my journey, the Lord brought me to a deeper brokenness and a more profound sense of meeting Him face-to-face. Each round with God ended in the death of something old and the birth of something new. Every encounter deepened God's anointing on my ministry.

THE BREAKDOWN

Let me share the story of my most profound experience of surrender to the Lord and the revolutionary consequences it had for me as a person. I was wrapped up in my normal cycle of continual meetings and appointments. When I started at Salem Church, I quickly fell into a life of hyperactivity. I was still finishing my work at Hood Theological Seminary. I was caring for a growing church of three hundred members and still working full-time at a funeral home. My position at the home required being on call twenty-four hours a day. A usual week involved forty to fifty hours of work on site.

To complicate matters, there was limited staff at the church, and I found myself doing nearly everything. I spent at least another thirty to forty hours a week meeting the needs of my growing congregation. My personal prayer and Bible reading ebbed. Fatigue robbed my sporadic devotions of any vitality. My ability to concentrate waned. For three years, I felt stretched thin as piano wire. On top of all that, I struggled to be an adequate husband to my wife, Harriet, and father to our little girl!

How much time do you give to personal prayer and Bible study?

My situation was getting desperate. I began flirting with the temptation of moving back to New York. Several prominent urban churches were courting me, and the idea of a large metropolitan pastorate was flattering. It was well known that urban churches really took care of their senior ministers. Here was opportunity for security, affluence, and the kind of prestige most young black pastors only dreamed of!

My heart, eyes, and ambition started to drift northward. At one point I was the prime candidate for four churches! Incredibly, not one door of opportunity opened for me—the prime candidate, and no one gave me a final call! I was devastated. I got angrier and angrier with God as He slammed door after door shut.

Then the Lord whispered inaudibly to my heart. "Anthony, if you will follow Me with your whole heart, I will bring New York to you."

I have always been what the older folks called a go-getter. I was driven. I set goals, and I moved in a straight line until I reached them. People and things got out of my way or were carried along by my momentum. I didn't stop until I got where I wanted to go.

With my desire to go to New York thwarted by God Himself, I threw myself even more deeply into my work at Salem. My love for the funeral profession and for the church held me tight. I couldn't let go of either. At that point, I knew that my call to the ministry was the most important for me, but I had two "mistresses" and couldn't let go of either one. The problem was that they both wanted me full-time! I was a workaholic, slaving around the clock with few breaks. I never took vacations and rarely a day off. Then, one Sunday morning, my world collapsed.

In the fall of 1984, I was pushing myself through the Sunday services at the end of a frantic week. After preaching my morning sermon, I simply blanked out and collapsed in the pulpit. Paramedics rushed me to Mercy Hospital. At the ripe age of twenty-seven, I had a massive nervous breakdown.

I was put into intensive care for two days. Doctors ran a number of tests to see if I'd had a stroke or heart attack. After the initial tests, my doctor recommended complete bed rest while the hospital assessed my daily progress. The attending physician told my wife that he really couldn't understand what was happening. It appeared that I was suffering from a massive reaction to stress, but it was affecting my heart rate and even my blood chemistry! The only possible treatment was an IV for dehydration and complete isolation.

For one week I could not recognize anyone, not even my wife or daughter. I actually don't remember a thing that happened to me that whole week. After a week in the hospital I became aware of my surroundings. I regained awareness slowly and wasn't very communicative.

One day, when I was awake but drifting in a blurry, dreamlike state, I thought I heard the sound of running water, like a gently moving stream. Then I felt a cool breeze and became aware of bits of a conversation. "I brought you by still waters." It was the Spirit of God. "The choice is up to you. Will you decide to follow Me totally? Walk with Me, and you will experience things you never dreamed possible. I will open doors for you to places you never thought you would go. You will be brought into the company of great people. Your ministry will be blessed! Trust Me!"

I could not speak or respond—I had to rest and listen! It was unlike any experience I had ever had with God. There in that hospital room, the Holy Spirit invited me to surrender entirely, and I accepted His offer. The modern-day Jacob had been to Jabbok. Anthony Jinwright was in intensive care!

This encounter with God probed a deep personal nerve. I had started my ministry at Salem with a fierce determination to be financially independent from the church, and my conviction had deep emotional roots. Bi-vocational ministry has been a strong cultural expectation in much of the black church community.

Few churches can pay a livable salary and, in my culture, ministers can be financially held hostage by the church.

I knew a number of ministers who had died with wounded hearts because of their congregation's ongoing lack of concern for their financial needs. When the church held complete control of the purse strings, the pastor was at the mercy of the people. My income from the funeral home provided me with dignity and some optional security. I leveraged it in politically testy situations.

So I had unrelentingly held tight to this source of self-dependence and security in my life. Now God was dealing again with the issue of who would be boss. This time the game was for keeps. Was I going to follow my call to ministry or go with the funeral home?

Although it was a struggle, I knew I had to obey the Lord. He was right; I could do only one thing effectively. That day I chose to serve the Lord, even if it meant limping financially for the rest of my life (Genesis 32:30–31).

But remaining faithful to this call was trying. In fact, when it came down to it, I couldn't do it. You have to understand how deeply I struggled with issues of control. Whether my problem was fear of **WILL YOU LET GO AND LET GOD TAKE CONTROL?** peer rejection or my love for the funeral profession (or some of both), I just couldn't let go of the steering wheel of my life.

Soon I found myself falling into the old habits of overwork and overcommitment. Although I'd promised to let God take control, my actions were leading me down the old road. I even began to work at the funeral home again. I loved the funeral business. Besides the second income, it provided me with opportunities to help people in times of crisis.

Finally, I had a slight relapse of my nervous break-down. It was a wake-up call from God. This was a life-and-death matter. I had made a decision, and I needed to focus my heart on following the Lord completely. This prayer of A. W. Tozer clearly sums up my feelings at that time:

> Father, I want to know Thee, but my coward heart fears to give up its toys. I cannot part with them without inward bleeding, and I do not try to hide from Thee the terror of the parting. I come trembling, but I do come. Please root from my heart all those things which I have cherished so long and which have become a very part of my living self, so that Thou mayest enter and dwell there without rival. Then shall Thou make the place of Thy feet glorious. Then shall my heart have no need of the sun to shine in it, for Thyself will be the light of it, and there shall be no night there. In Jesus' Name, Amen (1948, 31).

A revolution began. I resigned from the funeral home and invested my extra time into deepening my life of prayer and study. I told my church about my encounter with God and my decision to rely wholly on Him. At first, I was afraid that they would criticize my desire to focus fully on my pastoral duties. To my amazement, the leadership was overwhelmingly supportive. God had already been working in the hearts of these wonderful people, and they had wanted for months to take me on as full-time pastor. But they knew of my love for the funeral business, so they kept quiet out of respect for me. God had had this blessing waiting for me for a long time, but I was blinded by my self-reliant stubbornness.

God set right to work making me into my calling. The Bible became a living Book to me; I feasted on the Bread of Life for personal nourishment, and not just for sermon ideas. I began to delve into Scriptures and put my faith in God's promises. I trusted Him to take care of me.

I became, in the words of the Skin Horse, "real." My mannerisms and behavior became marked by a new brokenness and humility. I was a spiritual pacesetter for my congregation. I became more sensitive to people and more concerned about their lives and their spiritual well-being. I was finally functioning as the shepherd of the flock!

The church began to prosper economically, and we decided to add church staff. This freed up more of my time, which I reinvested into more prayer and sermon preparation. As the church grew, I was able to spend even more time in prayer and devotion. And, thanks to my changing heart, my preaching improved! I spoke with more unction and power, with deeper meaning and resolve. Theory and conjecture dissolved into an ocean of firsthand knowledge of the spiritual life. Now I spoke of what I knew to be true, and God began to soak my words in His anointing. My ministry changed because my life changed.

RISE UP FROM THE MUD

I've shared my story to help you understand how God changes our character before He gives us the anointing.

THE CROSS IS ESSENTIAL TRAINING FOR THE ANOINTED LIFE.

Hopefully, you can see how the Lord wants to work through your brokenness. What trials and difficulties are you facing? Do you understand that through them Jesus is pursuing you relentlessly in love? Mud wrestling with the Lord is probably not your best option. Surrender is the key.

Submitting to God's loving discipline is never easy; the cross can be painful when it's killing your old self-security and sense of control. But it is essential training for the anointed life. God wants to work a deeper sense of dependency and surrender in your life. Don't be afraid! He is planning to bless you.

It might seem as if God doesn't play fairly. Remember the dirty trick He used on Jacob? He may use the most painful experiences of your life. But let me point out that the hardest stone requires the hardest chisel. Make yourself soft in His hands, and watch Him craft you into a vessel to hold His anointing!

> When God wants to drill a man
> And thrill a man
> And skill a man,
> When God wants to mold a man
> To play the noblest part;

When He yearns with all His heart
To create so great and bold a man
That all the world shall be amazed,
Watch His methods, watch His ways!
How He ruthlessly perfects
Whom He royally elects!
How He hammers him and hurts him
And with mighty blows converts him
Into trial shapes of clay which
Only God understands;
While his tortured heart is crying
And he lifts beseeching hands!
How he bends but never breaks
When his good He undertakes;
How He uses whom He chooses
And with every purpose fuses him;
By every act induces him;
To try His splendor out—
God knows what He's about (Sanders 1994, 141)!

QUESTIONS FOR REFLECTION AND DISCUSSION

1. In what ways has the Lord worked in your life to bring about brokenness? How has brokenness affected your openness to Him?

2. Are there ways you strive to maintain control of your life and ministry? What is your area of greatest insecurity? How has guarding it contributed to problems in your life? What would you have to give up for God to have total control?

3. Has Jesus ever met you by the riverside? Describe the time in your life you felt God speaking to you most clearly about your relationship to Him. How did this encounter affect the way you live every day?

CHAPTER SIX

PERSONAL DEVOTION AND THE ANOINTING

PERSONAL DEVOTION AND THE ANOINTING

The most important and permanent change that came through my emotional breakdown and recovery was in my prayer life. When I came out of that time, I was very committed to a consistent, intense life of prayer.

I've stayed true to that commitment, but it hasn't come easily or naturally to me. Like most pastors, I'm constantly pressed for time. Not only that, but I have a public role to fill. It's tempting to spend my energy in meeting other people's expectations. When I do, I earn immediate praise and can bask in the approval of the people around me. So, in some ways, it's much harder to quietly sit in God's presence, praying and worshipping. No one notices that!

I find it's even more difficult to have a healthy prayer focus when I'm constantly exposed to popular culture. I like the way Terry Muck described the situation:

> We live in a culture that discourages prayer. We are a mechanized, secularized society. We are surrounded by appliances that satisfy our every culinary need, home entertainment devices that stimulate our senses both good and bad, transportation possibilities that take the sting out of travel, and working with tools that makes *labor* a misnomer. This ease of satisfying want and whim is what make prayer so difficult. Prayer, the essence of which is obedience and submission, runs counter to a culture where we are beholden to very few. Further, some cultures in history have revolved around the church and the monastery. Ours doesn't. We live in a secular culture where man, not God, is the measure of all things (1985, 25).

In other words, while the anointed life is about being, not doing, our society focuses completely on doing. As a result, busyness is our biggest enemy. Our responsibilities and hobbies don't only crowd out our time with God—they make us look and feel as if our lives are rolling along nicely. It's possible to live an adequate Christian life but fall far short of the anointing God has for you. Eugene Peterson described the difference as it applies to his preaching:

> I have no interest in "delivering sermons," challenging people to face the needs of the day, or giving light, inspirational messages. With the help

provided by scholars and editors, I can prepare a fairly respectable sermon of either sort in a few hours each week, a sermon that will pass muster with most congregations. They might not think it the greatest sermon, but they will accept it.

But what I want to do can't be done that way. I need a drenching in the Scriptures; I require an immersion in biblical studies. I need reflective hours over the pages of Scripture as well as personal struggles with the meaning of Scripture. That takes far more time than it takes to prepare a sermon.

I want the people who come to worship in my congregation each Sunday to hear the Word of God preached in such a way that they hear its distinctive note of authority as God's Word, and to know that their lives are being addressed on their home territory. A sound outline and snappy illustrations don't make that happen (1998, 20–21).

Don't think that this applies only to preachers! I'll bet you rarely miss time with God because you're busy doing something wrong. More likely, your quiet time gets squeezed out of existence by important projects that "somebody had to do." Maybe you had a terrific idea yesterday. Let's say you bought tickets to take your son to a hockey game this weekend—no reason, just to tell him you love him. Great job! (Let's hope you're that thoughtful with your wife!)

DOES YOUR TIME WITH GOD GET SQUEEZED OUT BY OTHER TASKS?

But if you'd had time to spend in prayer, releasing the anointing in your life, maybe God would have told you that your son has been waiting all week for you to come home in time for dinner. Maybe you would have noticed that slight stoop in his shoulders. It's new, you know, and it's not just the teen years setting in. There's a bully at school who's been tearing his self-esteem to shreds, and he just wants to be able to talk to you over a normal meal...and maybe shoot baskets in the driveway for a while afterward.

As my own nervous breakdown proved, having too many "good things" can be very bad for you—and God may let you sprint headfirst into a concrete wall if that's the only way to stop you!

LIFE IN THE SECRET PLACE

It's absolutely essential that you resist the pressure to neglect your prayer life. Your ability to live in God's anointing is dependent on the time you spend with Him. The great preachers of history were typically people of deep and earnest prayer. They all learned the power of time alone with God. As E. M. Bounds put it, "The ability to talk to people is measured by the ability...[to] talk to God for people" (Bounds 1997, 571). Scripture is rich with examples of how God met with His servants in solitude, sometimes in secret places.

Jacob met God in the countryside at Bethel. His father, Isaac, and grandfather, Abraham, had met with Him on top of Mount Moriah. God called Moses on the backside of the desert, speaking to him from a burning bush. Later, on Mount Siani, He gave Moses the greatest revelation in the Old Testament, revealing His will for Israel and allowing Moses to see Him—at least His *"back parts"* (Exodus 33:23)—with his physical eyes.

Those were all places of glory, revelation, and communion with God. But they were rare, special occasions. God wanted to meet with His servants on a regular basis. He gave Moses specific instructions for building a temple that could travel with the Israelites. He called it a *tabernacle,* which means "tent of meeting." While it was being constructed, God met with Moses in a provisional tent of meeting, and they talked (Exodus 34:34). The continuing presence of God, manifested as a pillar of cloud first at the provisional tent and later at the tabernacle, was a sign to the Israelites (and to the nations around them) that God's anointing was with them. At times, after Moses spent time with God, his face glowed with a supernatural light, and he wore a veil afterward so that people could look at him without being blinded. (See Exodus 34:29–35.)

Other great Israelite leaders also met God in the secret place. It was in the tabernacle at Shiloh that young Samuel first heard the Lord's call (1 Samuel 3:2–4), and God continued to meet him there (v. 21). David, king and inspired psalmist, longed for times of solitude spent in God's house. By the middle of his life, he wrote that his greatest desire was to dwell in the house of the Lord for the remainder of his days (Psalm 27:4). David discovered the tabernacle as a place of intimacy and power (vv. 3–6). The sanctuary of the Lord inspired David with a spiritual vision of God's glory. No matter where he was—fighting in battle or fleeing in exile—David hungered and thirsted for his times in God's presence (Psalm 63:1–2). For the embittered Asaph, entering into the sanctuary was the thing that settled his discordant heart. In the secret place, God provided the revelation that quieted his struggle to understand the unfairness of life (Psalm 73:17).

Living Water

Under the old covenant, the Jews observed a holy festival called the Feast of Tabernacles. It was very involved, but the point was to remind them that God had chosen them, brought them out of slavery in Egypt, and promised to live with them and care for them. On the final day of this celebration, the high priest symbolically poured out a large pitcher of water. It was a reminder that one day God would pour the waters of salvation out on the faithful remnant of His people.

One year, on the last day of this festival, Jesus stood up and cried, *"If anyone is thirsty, let him come to me and drink. Whoever believes in me, as the Scripture has said, streams of living water will flow from within him"* (John 7:37–38 NIV). Jewish teachers usually sat when they taught, but Jesus stood up to make this announcement, indicating that He thought it was extremely important. Scripture is also clear that Jesus *"said* [this] *in a loud voice"* (v. 37). He jumped up and yelled!

The fresh spring of the anointing is within us.

Jesus identified Himself as the source of the living water, which is a symbol of the Holy Spirit. The implication is clear for new-covenant believers. We no longer rely on a prophet, priest, or king to commune with God in the tent of meeting. The spring of the anointing is within us! But Jesus said, *"Come to me and drink."* There is no substitute for time with God. Time spent in the secret place will be your source of God's anointing. E. M. Bounds explained:

> [Holy Spirit] anointing is not an inalienable gift. It is a conditional gift. Its presence is perpetuated and increased by the same process by which it was at first secured—by unceasing prayer to God,...by deeming all else loss and failure without it. This anointing comes directly from God in answer to prayer. Only praying hearts are filled with this holy oil. Only praying lips are anointed with this divine unction....Prayer, much prayer, is the sole condition of keeping this anointing.... Without perseverance in prayer, the anointing, like overkept manna, breeds worms (1997, 509).

Everything you accomplish should be secondary to a childlike sense of acceptance and freedom before the Lord. Too many Christians struggle with feelings of failure and burnout because they emphasize the things they're doing instead of the person they are becoming.

When was the last time you spent time in unhampered conversation with your heavenly Father? Time spent alone with God is never wasted. The secret place facilitates "doing" in a remarkable way. God's "time economy" works on the same principles as the rest of life—the more you give to Him, the more He prospers what you have left! When you spend sufficient time ministering to God, His anointing flows more easily through you for the rest of the day. The psalmist emphasized how futile it is to work without God's blessing:

*Unless the L*ORD *builds the house, its builders labor in vain. Unless the L*ORD *watches over the city, the watchmen stand guard in vain. In vain you rise early and stay up late, toiling for food to eat—for he grants sleep to those he loves.*

(Psalm 127:1–2 NIV)

The realization of this Scripture has led many Christians to say, "I have so much to do today that I must spend extra time alone with the Lord."

Life without spiritual intimacy is its own punishment. Either you will come to a place of true communication with God, or your Christian walk will atrophy to a collection of formalities. Time spent in the secret place has been the heart of my life for years now. Communion with God directly shapes my identity and behavior. My sense of identity is forged and sustained in the hours I spend in personal prayer. He reminds me that I'm His precious child, and the cry of "Father!" bubbles out of my soul, along with the fresh spring of His anointing. I spend a lot of time just being quiet before the Lord. It seems to help counter my tendency to become preoccupied with empty business.

Don't Check Your Brain at the Door

Please don't get the idea that solitude with God means switching off your brain and floating in a spiritual cloud. Christians have a tendency to think that working to understand the Scriptures is the opposite of getting to know the Spirit of God. This false separation is wrong and will cripple your anointing if you allow it. Someone once criticized the great theologian

B. B. Warfield for being too intellectual. "I think ten minutes on your knees will teach you more of true and deep knowledge of God than ten hours over your books," the critic said.

"What?" Warfield replied. "More than ten hours over your books *while* on your knees?" Warfield saw no division between spiritual and intellectual contact with God and His Word.

Paul advised Timothy,

> *Of these things put them in remembrance, charging them before the Lord that they strive not about words to no profit, but to the subverting of the hearers. Study to show thyself approved unto God, a workman that needeth not to be ashamed, rightly dividing the word of truth. But shun profane and vain babblings: for they will increase unto more ungodliness.* (2 Timothy 2:14–16)

As leader of the church in Ephesus, Timothy was responsible for steering the people away from teachings and debates that did not reflect God's character—things that would *"increase unto more ungodliness."* But how was he to understand God's character for himself? Not by increasing his prophetic discernment. Paul made himself very clear: Have a good work ethic about studying Scripture. Learn how to handle the Word of Truth.

LEARN HOW TO HANDLE THE WORD OF TRUTH.

I understand why we have a hard time balancing study with intimate prayer, but it's actually a bit silly to believe that they are opposed to each other. When

Jesus promised to send the Holy Spirit, He said, *"But the Comforter, which is the Holy Ghost, whom the Father will send in my name, he shall teach you all things, and bring all things to your remembrance, whatsoever I have said unto you"* (John 14:26).

You see? Jesus put the intimate role of the Holy Spirit (*"the Comforter"*) in the same breath as the study of His character (*"shall teach you all things"*). They work together, and you can't have the fullness of one without the other. Cotton Mather, one of the great Puritan preachers, made himself a simple rule. While he was studying the Bible, he wrote out thoughts that he wanted to include in his sermons. Whenever he reached the end of a paragraph, he stopped his work to pray, meditate, and examine his heart by the truth he had just written (Kemp 1997, 123). Not all of your prayer times need to include Bible study. Jesus spent whole nights out on a hillside alone, just praying and listening to His Father. But you can't neglect the Word and still function in the anointing He has for you.

The New Testament is clear that, though He was God, Jesus grew and learned in the same way that all little boys do. But He knew the Scriptures better than most of us ever will. Here's an example:

Toward the end of His earthly ministry, Jesus was very unpopular with the various sects of Jewish teachers. They often tried to discredit Him by asking Him questions they thought He wouldn't be able to answer. They hoped that by embarrassing Him in public, they would be able to shut Him up.

One such sect was called the Sadducees. This group did not believe that there would be a resurrection of the dead at the end of time, and they rejected all the oral traditions of the Pharisees. They also refused to accept any of the prophetic Old Testament writings. They believed in the five books written by Moses, and no more. Though they were a small group, the Sadducees were very involved in the local government and had a lot of political power.

They challenged Jesus with the following story:

> *"Teacher," they said, "Moses wrote for us that if a man's brother dies and leaves a wife but no children, the man must marry the widow and have children for his brother. Now there were seven brothers. The first one married and died without leaving any children. The second one married the widow, but he also died, leaving no child. It was the same with the third. In fact, none of the seven left any children. Last of all, the woman died too. At the resurrection whose wife will she be, since the seven were married to her?"* (Mark 12:19–23 NIV)

You see Jesus' dilemma? He couldn't just tell them whose wife the lady would be at the resurrection, because the Sadducees didn't believe in a resurrection! It was a trick question. He had to address that issue first, or else He would have looked like a fool. But He couldn't use any of the traditional Scriptures about the resurrection, because the Sadducees didn't accept them as being from God!

To His followers, it must have looked as though Jesus was stuck. How could He give an answer that would satisfy the Sadducees without offending the Pharisees (who did believe in the resurrection)? But Jesus didn't even slow down to switch gears. He told them,

> *Are you not in error because you do not know the Scriptures or the power of God? When the dead rise, they will neither marry nor be given in marriage; they will be like the angels in heaven. Now about the dead rising—have you not read in the book of Moses, in the account of the bush, how God said to him, "I am the God of Abraham, the God of Isaac, and the God of Jacob"? He is not the God of the dead, but of the living. You are badly mistaken!* (Mark 12:24–27)

Jesus knew the Scriptures so well that He was able to use a very unlikely passage to demonstrate truth. The Sadducees had no way to argue with Him, because He used one of their favorite books of the Bible. And the Pharisees couldn't accuse Him of perverting God's Word to please the

THE ANOINTING WILL FLOW OUT OF INTIMACY WITH GOD.

Sadducees. In fact, I'll bet some of the Pharisees took mental notes for the next time they were in a debate with the Sadducees!

Jesus said, *"But the Comforter, which is the Holy Ghost, whom the Father will send in my name, he shall teach you all things, and bring all things to your remembrance, whatsoever I have said unto you"* (John 14:26). The anointing for your calling will flow out of a place of intimacy with God. In the secret place, He will teach you about His character and supernaturally change your heart to be like His. Study to become a skilled

Word-smith. Be open to receive the comforting embrace of your heavenly Father.

QUESTIONS FOR REFLECTION AND DISCUSSION

1. Describe what time in the "inner court" means to you. How has meeting with God privately prepared you to be the person He's calling you to be in public?

2. What are your biggest hindrances in maintaining a consistent and vital prayer life? What can you do to secure uninterrupted time alone with God?

3. What symptoms let you know that you're spending too much time doing, without enough focus on just being?

4. Have you been reluctant to spend "too much" time studying the Bible? What efforts can you make to follow Jesus' example of balancing study and personal communication with God?

CHAPTER SEVEN

BRINGING IT HOME

CHAPTER SEVEN

BRINGING IT HOME

Ahealthy emphasis on prayer and solitude doesn't give you the right to become a hermit, although I sometimes think that life would be a lot easier that way. The more God's character is developed in you, the more you will want to reach out to the hurting people around you. Balancing solitude and outreach requires discipline. That's why Paul often referred to his life as though it was a race. It requires intense, regular training and discipline. If you're sloppy in your private training, it shows in public. The anointed life is a marathon, not a sprint. Settle into your stride and let the Holy Spirit do His work in you—and through you.

I've learned a lot by experience over the years. Let me take the role of a coach at this point. Imagine me in a sweat suit, with a whistle around my neck and a clipboard under my arm. Let me share a couple of training secrets with you, and maybe I can give you a head start.

MAINTAIN A SERVANT'S ATTITUDE

You might be tired of my repeating this, but bear with me: Being is more important than doing. You are called to become like Christ, and He was, above all else, obedient to the Father. Learn to adopt a posture of utter surrender to God. In my times of personal prayer, I often lie down right on my face, to demonstrate my complete reliance upon the Lord. I cry intensely, "God, I want to be what You want me to be. I don't want to get outside of Your will."

This all-encompassing spiritual surrender was an important part of the two most famous prayers Jesus prayed. Listen:

> *Our Father which art in heaven, Hallowed be thy name. Thy kingdom come. Thy will be done in earth, as it is in heaven.* (Matthew 6:9–10)

> *O my Father, if it be possible, let this cup pass from me: nevertheless not as I will, but as thou wilt.* (Matthew 26:39)

So my first instruction to you as your coach is this: The anointed believer must surrender totally to God. This is a daily exercise. Cultivate your identity as God's servant. As His servant, your heart and eyes will focus on doing His pleasure in the mundane grind of everyday life.

I lift up my eyes to you, to you whose throne is in heaven. As the eyes of slaves look to the hand of their master, as the eyes of a maid look to the hand of her mistress, so our eyes look to the LORD our God, till he shows us his mercy.

(Psalm 123:1–2 NIV)

If I had not been obedient to get out of the funeral home business, do you think my preaching would have any anointing today? Do you think I would be a pastor at all? The truth is, I would be dead. Not just because of the medical condition that my life-style was causing, but because God's HOW CAN YOU KNOW THAT YOU'RE SUBMITTED TO GOD? presence would not be with me. I might have kept on breathing, but the man I am supposed to be would have died. Surrender to the Lord is the first priority for spiritual fitness.

But maybe God hasn't asked you to quit your job and become a traditional minister. Most people aren't called to do that. So how can you know that you're really submitted to Him? Are you sure that you have a servant's heart? Jesus said,

When the Son of man shall come in his glory, and all the holy angels with him...then shall the King say unto them on his right hand, Come, ye blessed of my Father, inherit the kingdom prepared for you from the foundation of the world: for I was an hungered, and ye gave me meat: I was thirsty, and ye gave me drink: I was a stranger, and ye took me in: naked, and ye clothed me: I was sick, and ye visited me: I was in prison, and ye came unto

me. Then shall the righteous answer him, saying, Lord, when saw we thee an hungered, and fed thee? or thirsty, and gave thee drink? When saw we thee a stranger, and took thee in? or naked, and clothed thee? Or when saw we thee sick, or in prison, and came unto thee? And the King shall answer and say unto them, Verily I say unto you, Inasmuch as ye have done it unto one of the least of these my brethren, ye have done it unto me.
(Matthew 25:31, 34–40)

John explained,

If anyone says, "I love God," yet hates his brother, he is a liar. For anyone who does not love his brother, whom he has seen, cannot love God, whom he has not seen. And he [God] has given us this command: Whoever loves God must also love his brother. (1 John 4:20–21 NIV)

In other words, you have to make a lifestyle out of walking what you talk. Obedience leads to the integrity that God wants to have in His people. As an old proverb put it, "If a man's life be lightning, his word will be thunder."

Ray Comfort tells about running into a group of teenagers at an airport. They were typical punks, with tight clothes, crazy hair, unprintable vocabularies, and enough metal jewelry to stock a small hardware store.

Ray struck up a conversation with them, and then gave them copies of an evangelical tract. To his surprise, they started reading them right there. Partway through, one of them commented that he didn't think adultery and theft were such terrible things.

"Your conscience knows right from wrong," Ray threw back.

"If I was hungry, I would steal food to live," the punk defended himself.

"If you're hungry, you should call me, and I'd feed you so you didn't have to steal," Ray said.

It turned out they *were* hungry, so Ray bought them all lunch. The teens were in shock, and one of them asked why Ray would do something like that.

He said, "Because I like you."

Instantly, they became so polite and grateful that Ray was embarrassed. And they took extra copies of the tract and promised to read them (Comfort 2002, 116–117).

Would you have the humility to tell a cocky, rebellious bunch of punks that you liked them? It would have been easy for Ray to say, "Because Jesus loves you." That would have kept him safely distant from them. It would have said, "I know Jesus, and you don't—so you need my help, and (since I'm such a nice guy) I'll help you." When Ray said, "I like you," he was putting himself on the same level with the punks. It meant that he respected their personalities. It meant that he appreciated their opinions. It meant that he was treating them the way Jesus treated the street people of His day.

Maybe when you come home from work next week, your wife will be at the peak of a busy day, and she won't really greet you properly. "Hi, honey. Can you take the trash out? I need some space in the kitchen, and that big box is really crowding things."

At that point, you'll have a choice. You've already done a full day's work. Your boss is a pretty important lady. For that matter, you handle a lot of responsibility yourself. People under you, and even people from other departments, look up to you. You're tired. And instead of being appreciated, you're getting demoted to garbage boy? You have a good reason to stand up for yourself! Or you can decide to show a servant's heart. Take a deep breath and ask the Holy Spirit to quiet you inside. When you set your briefcase down and toss your jacket over a chair, saying, "Sure, hon. What about the trash upstairs?" you'll have completed the first set of anointing exercises.

LISTENING TO THE LORD

The second training secret I want to share with you is about hearing God, and hearing Him correctly. Learning to recognize God's voice is very important THIS WORLD IS if you want to partner with the Holy FULL OF VOICES Spirit. This world is full of voices that THAT WILL will distract you from the anointing DISTRACT YOU. God has for you. One of those voices is probably yours! Don't let too much of your prayer life be a monologue. Fine-tuning your ability to recognize God's voice requires constant attentiveness.

I once knew a young Christian man, a student in college, who visited a Charismatic church. At one point, he was at the altar, praying and asking God for help. The minister began to pray for him, and then began using the gift of prophecy. He told the college student that God loved him, no matter how much he felt like a failure. The student began to weep, because he was so overwhelmed. God had noticed how hard he was trying!

But then the minister continued speaking, talking about how God offered forgiveness for all things, including sexual impurity. As he continued to talk about sexual issues, the young man grew more and more uncomfortable and began to wish that he could slip away. This particular young man wasn't battling with issues of purity at that time. He was struggling with his classes, he was playing in a band, and he felt like he couldn't keep up with any of the responsibilities God had given him.

The minister had slipped out of the anointing, and not because he was wicked or because he didn't care about the young man. The minister missed God's anointing just because he was not tuned in to God's voice.

Some years later, the same young man—now graduated from college and engaged to be married—found himself with the same feelings of failure. While riding on a church bus one day, he asked one of the elders from his church to pray with him. The elder prayed, and then began to prophecy, reminding the young man that God loved him no matter what. He went on to say that God was pleased with the young man—and then he stopped. In fact, the elder just backed away and let the young man talk to God alone. The young man left that bus holding his head up, and with a gleam in his eye. Why? Because the elder had been carefully tuned in to God's voice and had been responsible enough to treat the anointing with reverence.

The apostle Paul was very strict about how the prophetic gifts were to be used, and very clear about their purpose. *"He that prophesieth speaketh unto men to edification, and exhortation, and comfort"* (1 Corinthians 14:3). This is so serious that we're not really going to talk about using prophecy in the church setting. Let's just talk about the basics. An anointed life will revolve around your ability to hear what God has to say about *you.*

CHECKS AND BALANCES

You can cultivate your discernment by focusing your devotional life on prayer and meditative reading of the Bible. Ask God to help you find the truths that you need the most for your life right now. When you find a passage that seems written just for you, take time to meditate on it, and study to see whether God elaborated on "your" truth. Be open to ideas that might require you to change the way you think or live. They'll give you wonderful opportunities to do all your submission exercises!

When you feel as if God has given you a supernatural revelation or direction, be sure that you really understand what the Bible has to say on the subject. Scripture is the written voice of God, and supernatural revelation will always agree with it. For instance, God will never tell you to abandon your family, because the Bible says that *"if any provide not for his own, and specially for those of his own house, he hath denied the faith, and is worse than an infidel"* (1 Timothy 5:8).

But it is scripturally possible that God could call you to take your family with you into the mission field. How can you know? Walk through the next few checkpoints.

If your revelation is scripturally sound, ask yourself: Does this thought bring me a sense of deep peace? James 3:17 says, *"The wisdom that is from above is first pure, then peaceable."* You might not feel exactly calm about packing everything up and moving halfway across the world, but God's direction will give you a quiet assurance that flows deeper than your emotions.

Once you have peace with what you think is God's direction, seek godly council. *"Where no counsel is, the people fall: but in the multitude of counsellors there is safety"* (Proverbs 11:14). Pray about it with your spouse—and really listen to what he or she has to say. Take it to your pastor, and to friends who have true maturity in Christ.

GOD'S DIRECTION WILL GIVE YOU A QUIET ASSURANCE AND PEACE.

Finally, pray long and hard about the timing. God anointed David to be king before he killed Goliath. And David waited for years after he killed Goliath—at first serving King Saul, and then hiding in the hills from the king's murderous jealousy. Through all that time, David refused to rise up and take the kingdom away from Saul. He probably could have staged a successful coup; he was much more popular (at least, until Saul put a bounty on his head), and he had a squad of crack soldiers that would put the Army Rangers to shame. But David waited, because he trusted God's timing.

Don't be afraid to sit on the things God tells you. I have found that, even when I have to wait for years, all God's promises come true, and His directions always lead me into His blessing.

Maintaining these disciplines has enriched and empowered my entire life. Above all, they have been a pathway for a deepening relationship with Jesus. My relationship with the Spirit has been an upward spiral. It began with my desperate sense of need for God, which drove me to seek Him in intensely personal prayer. This time of abiding in His presence slowly began to change my heart. My family and congregation sensed the fresh presence of God in me, and they responded to it. This only drove me to deeper prayer. Deeper dependency on God created deeper intimacy with God. *Waiting on the Lord is the key factor in finding the anointing.*

Questions for Reflection and Discussion

1. How would you describe the adequacy of your "spiritual fitness program"? What spiritual disciplines do you practice regularly? Which of these is related most directly to what God is doing in your life right now?

2. In what areas of your life do you seem to fail to hear God's voice? How could you better open these areas to the leading of the Spirit?

3. Do you maintain a balance between study of God's Word and time on your knees (or on your face) before God? What can you learn from Jesus' example?

4. In what situations or circumstances in your life do you think you could allow the anointing to flow through you in greater power?

CHAPTER EIGHT

THE MOMENT OF TRUTH

The Moment of Truth

The band erupts into an energetic anthem. The ceremonial entrance has begun. The matador marches into the stadium proudly and steadily. His head is raised and his eyes fixed straight ahead, as though he doesn't notice the enthusiastic fans. He is flanked by the *cuadrilla,* a group of his apprentices who will learn from his skill—or from his mistakes.

The matador has practiced his moves and rehearsed his strategies for days. He has thought over every detail a thousand times, and then, as he slipped into his uniform, he has cleared his mind. Now he stands alone in a stadium of thousands. His focus is complete. The door stands in front of him, with *el toro* behind it. The red cape is draped over his arm. His strong, light sword extends firm and friendly from his sweating palm. He stands poised, but relaxed, his whole being absorbed in the moment as he draws each breath. The door swings open, and nothing from the past matters. There is no future. Only now.

Like the matador, you've rehearsed and strategized, maybe for years, to win others to Christ. But what do you do when the moment arrives? When you're at work, at home, or even at the grocery store, are you focused on how the Spirit is leading you?

Steve walks by your desk for the fourth time today. You know his mother passed away just last week, but he seems cheerful enough. He must be coping well. So why can't you shake the feeling that you should offer to pray with him? You look around. There's no way you could do it without people noticing. You know that Bill Brice, across the aisle, is a young Christian. Will he think you're trying to show off how holy you are?

You've prayed hundreds of times for the "lost souls" in your city. You've toyed with volunteering at a soup kitchen some Saturday, when you get the time. You pray almost daily for God to use you, right where you are. Now you stare at your work without really seeing it. You try to clear your mind, but can't help thinking. Steve heard you swear a couple months ago. You slipped and dropped that stack of papers down the stairs...and then your tongue slipped. What if he laughs you off, and then tells everyone that you're a phony?

It seemed so easy at the altar, where you prayed for God to give you an anointed life. And after the way He's been changing your attitudes at home, and the time you've spent alone with your Bible, you thought you were ready for anything. It's only at the moment of truth that you remember something key: You can't make the anointing happen. You might not even be able to work up the guts to go pray with Steve, unless God lends you His grace.

If you've allowed God to begin rearranging your mental furniture, and you've committed to spending time just to get to know Him, then you've taken the first important steps toward living the anointed life. The ability to finish strong is directly proportional to your ability to partner with the Holy Spirit.

RIDING SHOTGUN WITH GOD

What do I mean by "partner with the Holy Spirit"? Well, many things are part of a Spirit-led, anointed life. Integrity. Caring for your family. Being active in the gifts of the Spirit. Being a witness. You could buy stacks of books to teach you how to do these things. You could take classes and memorize appropriate responses to every situation imaginable. But you have to live in the real world, with real people. Your spouse alone can— and will—say or do things that go far beyond the situations you could imag-ine while reading a book. Then what will you do? How should you respond to a tone of voice you've never heard before...especially in front of the kids? Are you sure that there isn't really something else underneath the issue at hand? Should you try to talk, or just listen for a while?

MANY THINGS ARE PART OF A SPIRIT-LED, ANOINTED LIFE.

The average person has two choices: guess, or just give up. Giving up isn't an option if you're serious about the anointed life. But guessing is pretty dangerous. Assuming that you know what's really bothering someone is usually a good way to upset him further, especially if you're wrong! You need another option. That option is partnering with the Holy Spirit.

David prayed, *"Set a watch, O Lord, before my mouth; keep the door of my lips. Incline not my heart to any evil thing"* (Psalm 141:3–4). This prayer—or the desire that this prayer is based on—is a basic part of any partnership with the Holy Spirit. If you give Him permission, the Holy Spirit will slam the "doors" of your mouth on ungodly words. Time and again, my temper has flared at the things people have done or said. I have a pretty good wit, and, given half a chance, I could cut just about anyone down to size. But no sooner do I start to open my mouth than a supernatural calm hits my heart like a cup of cold water in the face, and I hear the Spirit murmur, "Hush."

I've never regretted obeying that voice. More than that, I'm often very thankful to be saved from the problems that my sinful human nature could cause me. And, best of all, the Holy Spirit isn't just an insurance partner, saving me from myself. Listen to what Jesus promised: *"And when they bring you unto the synagogues, and unto magistrates, and powers, take ye no thought how or what thing ye shall answer, or what ye shall say: for the Holy Ghost shall teach you in the same hour what ye ought to say"* (Luke 12:11–12). In other words, even in situations where your back is up against the wall, the Holy Spirit is a strong partner who always has the right words to say. This is one reason why it's so important for you to learn how to recognize His voice. When you know for sure that your Partner is with you, you can do the impossible!

> *If any of you lack wisdom, let him ask of God, that giveth to all men liberally, and upbraideth not; and it shall be given him. But let him ask in faith, nothing wavering. For he that wavereth is like a wave of the sea driven with the wind and tossed.*
>
> (James 1:5–6)

Songwriters Steve Taylor and Peter Furler described partnership with the Spirit this way in a song by the Newsboys entitled "Spirit Thing":

> It pushes when I quit.
> It smells a counterfeit.
> Sometimes It works a bit like a teleprompter…
> It's here to guard my heart.
> It's like a holy nudge.
> It's like a circuit judge in the brain.

That describes the interplay of wisdom and discernment that the Holy Spirit brings to the table. Your part is to bring an open heart and a humble attitude. Paul called it *"your spiritual act of worship"* (Romans 12:1 NIV).

THAT'S WORSHIP?

Modern Christian culture is placing a lot of emphasis on worship. It's wonderful to be reminded so strongly that corporate worship is a meeting with God Himself. For the first time in generations, we are seeing the ways in which the Holy Spirit responds to passionate, intimate worship. We are learning to bless the Father's heart.

Unfortunately, we are also learning that there is great danger in forgetting what the word *worship* means. Most people have begun to think that worship means "getting together to sing," or a special kind of music.

Worship is more than music. It's a way of life. There has even arisen a worship music industry that attempts to sell worship encounters, neatly pressed on CDs! Matt Redman, a worship leader whom God has used powerfully in England and the United States, once saw a songbook being sold as "the forty most powerful worship songs of today." He commented, "Who told them that? Was it God? How nice of Him to reveal His forty favorites so that a book could be marketed effectively" (Redman 2001, 91)!

Obviously, there is an important place for worship songs. The Bible is clear that God loves it when His children use music to express their devotion to Him. But we have somehow begun to treat it like an art, instead of the spiritual reality it should be. As a result, most people never work at maintaining the open heart and humble attitude they need in order to partner with the Holy Spirit. Bible scholar Jason Labonte said,

> The Greek words used for *worship* convey falling to one's knees in reverence, giving an act of service, or declaring praise. Every breath we take should be an act of worship. Our lives should be lived in reverence. Our minds should *"pray without ceasing"* (1 Thessalonians 5:17)....So, in that sense, we need to be living a worship experience.

Allow me to summarize what I've said so far in this chapter. To partner with the Holy Spirit requires that we adopt a lifestyle of worship. That doesn't mean that we never stop singing, but that everything we do acknowledges the lordship of Jesus Christ and is humbly open to God. Obviously, this is something we must learn. Remember learning to ride a bicycle? The process wasn't complicated: You got on, did your best to keep your balance, fell off, and got back on again. It was the same with the multiplication table—you tried, got it wrong, and kept trying until you could consistently get it right. What was your secret? How did you do it? Practice.

Imagine that you're learning to fly a private plane. At this point, you have spent hours in classes, learning how your airplane works. You've learned to trust your instruments, instead of your feelings. (In the dark, without instruments, a pilot can think he's flying straight and level while he's in a spiraling nosedive.) You've spent hundreds of hours in the safety of the training plane, watching and learning under the guidance of your instructor. Now, for the first time, you're up in the air all alone, and it's time to come in for a landing—the first landing you've made without the instructor's hand hovering by the stick. Today, he's in the control tower, and your success depends on how well you can both listen to him and interact with your plane.

You're nosing down, decreasing your altitude, when the plane starts to shake. "We have a northeast wind of about eight knots down here at ground level," he tells you. "You'll need to compensate for that on your approach." You do, and the shaking eases to a quiver as your propeller bores a hole in the approaching cold front.

"Now, a touch more rudder, and start backing off the throttle," your instructor says. A touch more rudder? You press gently, thinking that you had enough rudder the first time. WHOMP! Your wheels bounce off the runway, jolting the plane back into the air. The throttle! You forgot to ease off on the throttle. Preoccupied by your questions over the last instruction, you momentarily closed your mind to the instructor's voice. WHOMP! You bounce again, like a drunken kangaroo on a rusty pogo stick.

"That's okay. Give it the juice, and pull out of there." Your instructor speaks quietly in your earphones. You pull up, climbing for the sky. Now, what do you think your instructor will do?

We often expect God to say, "Well, you blew it. You obviously can't be an anointed Christian. You just don't listen. I don't know why I wasted my time with you. Go crash in a field somewhere—I'll find someone better." But God doesn't say that, just as your instructor doesn't say that. See, he is a pilot, too, and he knows how hard it is to keep your mind focused when you're in the middle of everything. He just says, "Bring it around for another go. Listen close now, and keep your eyes open."

Therefore, since we have a great high priest who has gone through the heavens, Jesus the Son of God, let us hold firmly to the faith we profess. For we do not have a high priest who is unable to sympathize with our weaknesses, but we have one who has been tempted in every way, just as we are—yet was without sin. Let us then approach the throne of grace with confidence, so that we

138

*may receive mercy and find grace to help us in
our time of need.*   (Hebrews 4:14–16 NIV)

So the next time you come in for a landing, you have
a little less confidence in your own ability and more
respect for your instructor's voice. When he tells you,
"Less rudder this time; the wind's dying back to about
three knots," you ease off the rudder pedal. And when
he says, "Don't throttle back too soon; you're probably a
little jumpy now," you take a deep breath and wait until
he says, "Okay, start backing off on the throttle." And
then, voila, you're rolling smoothly down the runway,
and you're brimming with confidence in your instructor.

The psalmist said, *"I love the LORD, because he hath
heard my voice and my supplications. Because he hath
inclined his ear unto me, therefore will I call upon him
as long as I live"* (Psalm 116:1–2). The writer of this
psalm went on to explain that he had been in a desperate situation and was afraid that he wouldn't be able to
stand up under the pressure. In fact, he was hardly a
great example of faith. *"I was overcome by trouble and
sorrow"* (v. 3 NIV). *"I said in my haste, All men are liars"*
(v. 11). But when he prayed, the Lord protected him and
gave him a way out of the situation. Now he was able
to say, *"Precious in the sight of the LORD is the death of
his saints. O LORD, truly I am thy servant; I am thy servant, and the son of thine handmaid: thou hast loosed
my bonds"* (vv. 15–16).

That doesn't mean that God considers the death of
believers to be a valuable thing! It means that their lives
are valuable to Him, and He possessively guards the

right to decide when those lives should end. This was part of the Hebrew teachings, but now the psalmist knew it from experience. He couldn't fake that kind of openness and trust, and neither can you. Living every day with a mind-set that reverences God's goodness (that's worship) requires us to under-stand just how good He is. And that means we simply have to dedicate our-selves to learning. The more we see His grace working despite our weakness, the more we will be able to live in a state of worship. The more our hearts are open in worship, the more the Holy Spirit will be able to partner with us. And that partnership is the outward fruit of an anointed life.

GOD'S GRACE WORKS IN US DESPITE OUR WEAKNESSES.

You Might Get Shot At

In the wild days of America's West, towns were often under a rough kind of mob rule, until they were recognized as official settlements and provided with a U.S. marshal. By the time the marshal arrived, he was usually very unwelcome. People had their own ways of doing things (even if that meant the strong preying on the weak), and they didn't want to be interfered with. The process of gathering the law-abiding citizens and building an honest community became known as "taming" a town. It required courage, skill, integrity, a measure of political talent, and a certain amount of bullheadedness. The men who were best at it are still famous today: men like Wyatt Earp and Bat Matterson.

While a town was being tamed, a marshal's job was very dangerous. More than a few were shot, some of them from ambush. In fact, choosing to ride with, or hang out with, a marshal was a dangerous thing. It put the law-abiding citizen in danger of those who resented the law. If a crook couldn't get a clear shot at the marshal, sometimes he'd put a bullet in one of the marshal's supporters, as a warning.

Spiritually speaking, that's what the world is like today. Satan is called the *"god of this world"* (2 Corinthians 4:4), and it's a world in rebellion to the law of God. Jesus came to earth to fulfill the law, and the adversary couldn't touch Him. But if you choose to partner with the Holy Spirit, you're choosing to ride with Christ. Spiritually speaking, this means you might get shot at. Perhaps it will be only negative thoughts, fear of failure, or a personality conflict with someone you really love. Maybe you'll find yourself in financial difficulty, struggling to believe that God will provide for you. Maybe you'll find memories of your past everywhere you go, trying to tell you that Jesus' blood wasn't enough—that you're still dirty, and will always be dirty.

No matter what it is, don't be surprised, and keep opening your heart to God. *"Let us then approach the throne of grace with confidence, so that we may receive mercy and find grace to help us in our time of need"* (Hebrews 4:16 NIV). As you learn to partner with the Spirit, you will learn to be like Paul, who said,

> And he [God] *said unto me, My grace is sufficient for thee: for my strength is made perfect in weakness. Most gladly therefore will I rather glory in my infirmities, that the power of Christ*

may rest upon me. Therefore I take pleasure in infirmities, in reproaches, in necessities, in persecutions, in distresses for Christ's sake: for when I am weak, then am I strong.

(2 Corinthians 12:9–10)

The Anointed Life in Action

Steve walks by your desk for the fifth time today. You close your eyes for a moment. "God…I'm not sure how to do this, but I want to partner with the Holy Spirit today. Please make it obvious for me, okay?"

"Hey!" Your silent prayer gets interrupted—by Steve! He beckons you over. "I don't think I understand how these relate." He points to the information on his computer screen, and you discuss it with him.

"Okay, thanks a lot," he says quickly and turns back to his work.

"Uh, how are you doing, since your mom passed away? Can I pray with you?" You blurt it out in one breath, feeling stupid before you even finish.

"What? Here?" He looks around quickly, then waves a hand. "I'm good. Thanks any…" To your surprise, he stops, looking at your face. "Well…okay." He shrugs.

You grab a nearby chair and sit at the end of his desk, to make him more comfortable. You really have no idea what to pray, but the words just seem to come. When you finish and look up, his eyes are watery. "No one else has even asked how I was. Thanks for caring."

As you walk back to your desk, you realize again that true caring is the best witness there is. Listening to your Instructor really paid off. And next time, you'll be a little quicker about it.

QUESTIONS FOR REFLECTION AND DISCUSSION:

1. When was the last time you felt like the Holy Spirit was using you as His partner?

2. What role does worship play in your life? Have you ever thought about worship as being more than music? How does this affect the way you view your own attitudes toward God?

3. Describe a time you felt God was giving you specific directions. What was He telling you to do? What did you do and what happened?

4. Are you comfortable with the idea of a process? What can you do to help yourself accept failures as part of the learning process? Do you take enough time to recognize the progress you have made in partnering with the Holy Spirit?

5. When was the last time you felt like life was a spiritual fight? What was happening that made you sense spiritual warfare? How did you respond to it? What are the main ways that the devil attempts to discourage you? How do you prepare for his attacks?

CHAPTER NINE

TRUTH AT WORK

Truth at Work

George Matheson was one of the most powerful preachers of nineteenth-century Scotland. In 1886, he became pastor of St. Bernard's Church in Edinburgh. Some months into his ministry there, it came time for the church to take Holy Communion.

In the Scottish tradition, elders visited members of the congregation at home to sign them up for Communion. One of Matheson's parishioners was a woman who had lived for years in a cellar, under filthy conditions. But when an elder knocked at this woman's cellar door, he found her gone. After much effort, he tracked her down, finally locating her in an attic room. She was very poor; there were no luxuries. But the attic was as light, airy, and clean as the cellar had been dismal and dirty.

"I see you've changed your house," the elder said to the woman.

"Aye," she said, "I have. You can't hear George Matheson preach and live in a cellar."

That story excites me, because my personal calling is to be a preacher. If only the Holy Spirit would work that powerfully through me! The cry of my heart is to live an anointed life, and that's why I get such joy from telling my own testimonies of God's grace. I pray that they will encourage you in your journey.

YOU WANT ME TO PREACH ABOUT WHAT?

One day while at home, I caught a part of the *Oprah Winfrey Show*. She was talking about the homosexual lifestyle. Her permissive slant conveyed a broad tolerance for gays and lesbians. As I watched the interviews, the Lord started to burden my heart with a message about this pressing need. It was a message dealing with homosexuality. I struggled with the Lord. I felt very uncomfortable because I didn't want to embarrass anyone. Honestly, I also wanted to skirt anything that could create a controversy and upset our recent congregational growth. Salem Church was exploding with growth. Our services were packed. Our popularity was peaking. We were setting up extra chairs at every service. It got so crowded that we were afraid the city would fine us for building code violations! A pastor knows that when things are on a roll, you don't do anything to dampen the enthusiasm. And a message on homosexuality would definitely dampen the enthusiasm.

Submitting to the Lord, I told the Spirit, "You are going to have to prepare the house for this message. You are going to have to set it up in such a way that the people will hear my heart and know that I love them in spite of their sins." I didn't even want to mention this topic in the church service. It had all the potential of blowing up in my face. As I read the Scriptures and prayed, the Lord simply told me to tell our people that it was time to "come out of the closet."

Sunday came sooner than I wanted. As I stepped forward to speak the Word, I was downright scared. The church was packed—would it be empty next week? My mouth was dry, but I finally worked up the faith to begin speaking. I began slowly and sincerely. My first words were meant to create a sincere connection with my hearers. "I have not come today to embarrass or to push anyone away from the church because of your lifestyle or hang-ups. I have come at the prompting of the Holy Spirit to share a word of hope, a word that will rescue you from whatever you are bound by. The Lord asks only that you come out of the closet and deal with it."

WHEN TRUTH IS AT WORK, IT IS NOT ALWAYS COMFORTABLE.

I then went on to speak from Romans 1, and 2 Corinthians 5:17, telling the congregation that God views homosexuality as sin. My preaching moved to underscore that there is hope of deliverance for those who turn to the Lord. The moment of truth came as I concluded my message. I felt that the Lord wanted me to give an invitation. Now the Holy Spirit had to make good on the sermon. But what if I was wrong? What would happen if I gave the invitation and no one responded? I was anxious about the embarrassment I would feel in front of the church.

"People all over the world are coming out these days," I concluded. "People are coming out of the closet with their drug addictions, their alcoholism, and their sexual indiscretions. You can come out of the closet today, no matter what you are caught up in, and we will love you in Jesus!" I stopped and waited to see what would happen. For a moment the congregation was quiet and still. Suddenly, there was a rustle of movement. I saw people starting to get up and move toward the altar. In front of the whole congregation, broken, hurting men and women made their way out of their personal closets of shame and sin. At the altar of prayer, people began to find freedom in Christ.

As a result of that message, several people who were bound by a hidden lifestyle of homosexuality confessed their need for help. Today they are free and are following the Lord wholeheartedly. God used my obedience to create a turning point in their lives. One of the men has been discipled, called into the ministry, and now witnesses freely of the power of Jesus that set him free!

An Iceberg at Heart

May Francis had a hard, embittered heart. Hostility radiated off her. Her icy looks could freeze your heart. She projected a clear message: Keep your distance! This was understandable. May had grown up in a rough, abusive environment, so she adopted her angry demeanor as a way to protect herself. She created a shell of hostility to keep people away. Many times, she let her anger get the better of her, and she flattened people with a critical phrase or two.

May had been in the church for a number of years before I came to pastor. She had married a young man from Salem and started attending with her new husband. By the time I arrived, May Francis was about forty-five years old. Although she carried a chip on her shoulder, she managed to be on the inside of things at the church. She was active in the church choir, where she sang with a lovely voice.

As a new pastor, I felt it was my duty to reach out to this hardened saint. One day after service, I gave her a cheerful greeting and asked how she was doing. "Fairly well, Pastor," she snapped. Her words were civil enough, but I was taken aback by the edge in her voice. Undaunted, I began an onslaught of kindness, trying week after week to break down the wall of her harsh fortress. No matter what I tried, things didn't seem to improve. I was determined that this women was going to change. I knew that somewhere beneath that armor of ice she had a soft heart, and the Holy Spirit was going to reach it. I maintained a warm and outgoing attitude toward her, in spite of her repeated rejections.

After about a year and a half at Salem, I felt God leading me to begin a sermon series on church unity. I spent a lot of time talking about the secret of church unity— God's love. During this period of emphasis, I focused on 1 Corinthians 13 and preached about "falling in love with Jesus." Each week I shared ways people can learn to fall in love with Jesus. I also pointed out that falling in love with the Lord always creates a change in heart toward other people.

Sometime during this period, I noticed a distinct change in May Francis. Like the warm winter sun the day after a Carolina snow, the Spirit used the Word to melt this woman's icy heart. The love of God was available for her. She began to see that there was a better way to live. I suspect that—drawn to His love—she was beginning to spend time alone with her heavenly Father. One day after services, I saw May leaving the church, and I was almost knocked off my feet at what I saw. A smile creased her face! I knew then that God was working on her in a special way.

A few weeks later she stopped me after the service to talk with me, and (wonder of wonders!) she told me that she liked my message. Some time later, she gave me a quick hug before she left after church, and I knew then GOD'S LOVE IS AVAILABLE, NO MATTER WHO YOU ARE. that God had fully pulled down the wall of her anger. Through the power of the Holy Spirit, May Francis was completely transformed. She began to volunteer for church ministries besides the choir. Her newfound love for people was contagious, and it led her to share with others in a number of ways. The clincher came when, after a few years, May asked to be a part of the Pastor's Aid Committee. This special group has one mission: to support and care for the pastor and his family!

Recently I joked with May, something I could never have even tried to do before. "May Francis," I teased, "you were one mean lady. It's amazing to me how you have changed. Do you really like your life this way?"

"Pastor Jinwright," she confided, "I would never want to go back to how I was. I am so happy now!"

BREAKING THE BONDAGE OF ADDICTION

Debra Love grew up in Salem. Her family attended regularly, so she was actively involved in the children's ministry and Sunday school. As young Debra matured into adolescence, she began to blossom in the church. She joined the choir, and her brilliant smile and youthful enthusiasm made an immediate impact on the congregation. Then something started to go wrong. Debra's choice of friends began to shift, and she started to hang around with a rough group from her neighborhood. She got a taste of the world and thought it was sweet. I was impressed by the young woman and her love for God, but I sensed that she was living a compromised life. Although she still participated in church and sang in the choir, there was a deepening rift in her soul. At the age of twenty-one, this amiable young woman got hooked on drugs and left the church. She dropped out of sight.

For years, Debra was gone from Salem. Her drug addictions enslaved her. She couldn't function without her fix. Cocaine was her constant companion. She sold herself out in prostitution and crime to make sure she had enough cash to feed her growing habit. She did whatever she needed to, and her life continued to come apart. She could not keep a job. She married a man who also used drugs—the needle was the thin cord that held them together, until Debra divorced him.

Debra's mother was a faithful, prayerful woman. She labored in intercession for her wayward daughter. Regularly she would come to the altar and tell me the latest information about Debra. Then we would kneel together and petition the throne of grace for this straying woman. We believed together that Debra would return to the Lord and the church.

Then, one Sunday, I noticed a familiar face in the congregation. I couldn't place the face, until after the services when her mother told me that Debra had come back to church. She had become so emaciated from substance abuse that I didn't recognize her. For weeks afterward, Debra would appear, and then disappear again.

During that time, God led me to preach a series on restoration and reconciliation. I spoke over the course of several weeks regarding God's power to bring us back from the ravages of sin and disobedience. On one particular Sunday I used the Prodigal Son as a model of restoration. "Friends, the Lord receives you no matter what you have been involved in," I reminded the flock. "You may be having the far-country experience today. You might even be down in the pigsty, feeding with the swine. If you would only listen to the Father's cry for you to return and come to your senses, you can come back home! The Lord is faithful to receive you and forgive you."

As I preached from my heart and pleaded with the congregation, I suddenly realized that Debra was back again. For a brief moment I stared at her. She looked worn and gaunt. She was listening attentively, but when I caught her sunken eyes, she turned her head abruptly and broke eye contact. I looked for her when the service ended, but she had quickly left before the choir sang the closing chorus. Little did I know that the truth she gleaned from my message would save her life!

Debra went home after church and went on a drug binge for several days to ward off her feelings of guilt and shame. Then, unexpectedly, something went horribly wrong. It might have been a bad batch of cocaine, or else Debra miscalculated the amount she mixed. After a few moments, she started to shake. She began to panic when she realize she had overdosed. She knew that her heart could freeze within minutes, killing her before help could arrive. Struggling to the nearby phone, she called 911 for help. Prostrated helplessly on the floor, she waited to die. Then she heard Pastor Jinwright's voice. Bits of the Sunday message came back to her.

> THE TRUTH OF GOD'S WORD WILL SET YOU FREE.

"You can come back home! God is faithful to receive you and forgive you."

In her pit of despair, this young and desperate woman pleaded with God to intervene. "Lord, if You'll help me, I will surrender my life to You. I will give You all of my life." She gasped these last few words and then passed out into a coma.

Debra awoke in the side wing of an emergency room. She had a piercing headache, but she was alive. The paramedics had arrived just after she went unconscious. They had administered CPR and rushed her to the hospital. She was safe, but a few minutes more and she would have died. Shivering in her hospital gown, Debra wrapped her arms around herself and began to weep.

Tears flooded down her face as she remembered what happened and how God had put faith into her heart through the memory of my Sunday message. She had been away in the far country, but now Debra had come home.

Debra Love became a changed woman. She made good on her promise to get right with the Lord. She entered a rehabilitation program and got clean from drugs. Finally the day came when she returned to Salem.

I was one of the first to welcome Debra. I hardly recognized her. She had never been a big person, but now she was a lot thinner than I remembered. Drugs had taken a dreadful toll on her. I greeted her with a warm hug and told her she was back home. Debra planted herself firmly in Salem. After a while, she started to teach in the Saturday church-school. She went on to start a ministry for people who struggle with substance abuse. She poured herself into people bound by chemical addictions, and, as a result of her testimony and the anointing that rests on her life, scores of people have been changed. Her radiant life has become a vital part of our church.

Your Turn

"But wait," you protest. "You didn't do anything. All you did was stand up and preach! That's your job, isn't it?"

Exactly! It's my job to preach. All I did was preach. Just like any other pastor. And God radically changed lives. Why the difference?

The answer is in the anointing. These stories are only three occasions when my life was right before God, I was open to partnering with the Holy Spirit, and God did what no person could have done. Remember what I said way back in the introduction? I told you that this book wasn't for special people. It's not for super-evangelists or intercessors of the seventh heaven. It's for normal people. It's for you. The anointed life happens when you become desperate for the Holy Spirit to control who you are. Then, just go do your job. God will do the rest.

QUESTION FOR REFLECTION AND DISCUSSION

No matter who you are, God wants to anoint your "normal life." Are you praying that God will show you what that means for you?

CHAPTER TEN

STAYING FRESH AND FINISHING WELL

CHAPTER TEN

STAYING FRESH AND FINISHING WELL

L iving in the anointing is the great adventure of my life and calling. My partnership with God is constantly challenging me toward a deepening relationship with Jesus Christ. Anointed life is really a journey of discipleship. My daily companion on the way is the Spirit of Jesus. The goal we walk toward is the high, upward call of God in Christ (Philippians 3:14). My desire is to complete the course within earshot of the affirming words, "Well done, My faithful servant."

The path is often hard. It is littered with betrayals, dangers, temptations, and spiritual fatigue. Entering into the life of the anointing requires a commitment to prayer and humble submission to God's call. Maintaining an anointed life is like running a marathon. It requires the ability to cultivate regular spiritual renewal and long-term endurance. Anointed life calls the believer to stay fresh in order to finish well. This final segment will provide you with some crucial guidelines for the road ahead.

STAYING FRESH

Living as children of light in this dark world can be exhausting. A human being can maintain intensity for only so long before becoming physically and emotionally tired. When you're tired, you simply don't function well. As a result, you must develop strategies to restore your spiritual reserves and refresh a passion for the Word of God. Here are some things I do to help me focus on what's important without burning out. God will work with you to find the balance that's perfect for you, if you're open to His Spirit.

MAINTAIN SPIRITUAL FITNESS

To run the marathon of the anointed life, a believer must focus on spiritual formation and fitness. A vibrant devotional life is my highest priority and the daily source of renewal. Prayer is the secret to my ability to keep a creative and enthusiastic edge to everything I do. By this I mean establishing and maintaining periods of personal intimacy with the Lord in the inner court. As a result of an ongoing devotional life, Jesus has brought me innumerable times of refreshing through the gentle breezes of the Spirit (Acts 3:19).

KEEP PHYSICALLY FIT

I have been preaching at Salem Church for over twenty years. There have been numerous seasons of dryness. Sometimes, they came simply from my overextending my physical reserves. I am usually physically resilient, and a few days of rest is all I need to restore my vigor. But I don't take this for granted. As I get older, I find myself more easily fatigued. The life of a minister is sedentary, and it's easy to get soft and lazy, which always hurts my energy level. So I make a priority of maintaining a healthy weight and getting sufficient sleep each night. I've even hired a personal trainer to guarantee that I am at my physical best. The spiritual benefits can be surprising!

STAY INTELLECTUALLY STIMULATED

I am always amazed how a fresh thought or a new perspective can charge up my energy levels and make me excited again about learning. This requires a dedication to study and discussion. I read extensively. I also learn from structured educational experiences. Recently I completed a doctorate in ministry from Gordon-Conwell Theological Seminary as a way to continue my personal development and growth. Don't be afraid of new ideas, even if they contradict your faith! If you tackle your questions, God will lead you to the right answers, and you will find fresh life in "old" truths.

> NEW IDEAS THAT CHALLENGE YOUR FAITH CAN BE GOOD!

MAINTAIN YOUR LIMITS

I love preaching. It's my calling, and if I hadn't learned some things earlier in my life, I probably would have preached myself to an early grave. Now I establish clear boundaries and preach outside of my church only when the Lord gives me the green light.

Special occasions are wonderful. It is a great honor to be asked to speak at an emancipation service, a church anniversary, or a graduation. The African-American church especially thrives on these community events. When I was a young minister, I would fill my calendar with these social and religious opportunities. I never thought of declining an invitation. If my calendar was open, I would be there. I figured that I was called to preach, so any opportunity was a mandate from God. Today I seldom do these events, especially without a release from the Spirit to do it. Since partnering with the Holy Spirit, I speak at those occasions only when my Senior Partner gives me the okay.

As a preacher, I face the danger of "overpreaching," just as you may face the danger of overcommitting! If the Spirit does not give you grace for something, don't expect a significant spiritual outcome. You might fill a slot on a program, but chances are you won't be effective in the Lord, and you won't experience the refreshing of the anointing. When you regularly live in the anointing, you will begin to discern between genuine callings and things that are essentially a waste of time and energy.

You might be thinking that I am going a bit overboard, but I see this pattern in the life of the Lord Jesus. The earthly ministry of Jesus had a God-directed pace to it. You don't see Jesus being driven to teach or perform miracles at all times in all places. I imagine that Jesus could have preached and ministered nonstop, but He knew His limits. He demonstrated the wisdom of taking time alone with God. That was His first priority.

It's true that, at times, the Lord ministered exhaustively. Yet at other times, He strategically withdrew. He even taught His disciples the importance of regular spiritual retreats (Mark 3:7).

Jesus was moved by something more important than common sense and a realization of His own physical limits. The deeper reality was that Jesus recognized His spiritual boundaries and limits. The Son could do nothing of Himself. He did only what the Father showed Him to do (John 5:19). Jesus partnered with the Spirit. This relationship acts as a pattern for my working with the Spirit. I do only what the Lord directs. In that way I am assured that the anointing will be at work, and I don't wear myself to a frazzle.

SEEK OUT THE ANOINTING

One of my deepest needs as a preacher is to go places where anointed preaching occurs. You should never get to a place where you feel that you have "arrived" and can no longer learn from other people. More important, you should never reach the point where you think you don't need to receive blessing from anointed people.

This is why I love to attend conferences. I look for energetic events in which I can receive anointed ministry from other preachers. Conferences like these stimulate my mind and renew my spirit. I don't have speaking pressures on me at such events. I go and sit back with thousands of others and receive from God. Not only am I enriched by the scheduled speakers, but I'm also strengthened by my informal conversations at breaks and around meals. Fellowship with anointed Christians is vital.

The Importance of Finishing Well

The apostle Paul had a profound sense of the divine call. His whole life was turned around by His encounter with Christ on the Damascus road. As a result, Paul was driven to please Jesus by fulfilling the heavenly vision.

STRIVE TO FULFILL THE HIGH, UPWARD CALL OF CHRIST. He focused his life with the intensity of an Olympic athlete. He was bent on one thing—to fulfill the high, upward call of Christ (Philippians 3:14). He pressed on with the desire to finish well (2 Timothy 4:7). Finishing well is the critical goal of the call, but it seems like a rare accomplishment in Christianity today. People who don't backslide become weary, then listless, and finally lifeless. Thousands of Christians "go through the motions" every Sunday. Where is the anointing?

God asks for a faithful heart (1 Corinthians 4:2). Finishing well requires both commitment and forethought. If you aren't alert, you can begin to slip into areas of sin. The small sins will drag on you, making it harder to focus on the life God has called you to. That drag will make it easier to slip into a lukewarm state, where God can't really do anything with you. That's why the New Testament warns us over and over: Stay awake!

Pride

Pride should be a primary concern for every believer. It's one of the most subtle, but one of the most dangerous, weaknesses. People who are new to the anointed life are especially susceptible to pride, because it's surprisingly easy to forget that God is the power behind us. Never forget where the power comes from. Robe yourself in humility. The more effective your life seems to be, the more room there will be for pride. Don't value human praise too highly! A spirit of arrogance and pride is the first step down a terrible chasm.

MONEY

Give me neither poverty nor riches, but give me only my daily bread. Otherwise, I may have too much and disown you and say, "Who is the LORD?" Or I may become poor and steal, and so dishonor the name of my God.

(Proverbs 30:8–9 NIV)

Are you content when all your needs are provided for? Or do you find yourself always wishing for more? Many people worry and struggle, wanting a financial "buffer," so that they can feel secure about the future. But as the writer of the proverb said, once they feel secure, it becomes easier to forget about God.

If you have an abundance, learn to have a generous and giving heart. If you feel that you have too little, learn to be content. Holding on to money is always damaging to the anointed life, whether it's because you have so little of it, or because you have so much that it's hard to manage. Learn to let God worry about your provision! Without that on your mind, you'll be able to dig into the anointed life He has for you.

SEXUAL SIN

If you're not careful, the anointed life can be a solitary life. Your spiritual journey can isolate you from others who don't understand the "weird" elements in your life. Since companionship and understanding are basic human needs, feeling alone can make you vulnerable to sexual temptations you normally would not find appealing.

If you are married, it is especially important that you do your best, before God, to maintain a healthy, loving, and mutually supportive relationship with your spouse. It is nearly impossible to keep your thoughts (and the actions that follow) pure if you don't feel understood and supported by your spouse. God designed the marriage relationship to thrive on healthy sexuality, which depends on both friendship and heart-intimacy. If your marriage is weak for any reason, you will automatically find yourself looking (perhaps even unconsciously) elsewhere to fill your need for companionship.

Whether you are married or not, you need to flee temptation. Refuse to look at or listen to things that will lead you toward sin. (Notice I said "toward" sin, not just "into" sin.) Develop and maintain a network of friends who believe as you do—Christians who are striving for the anointed life and who understand your failures and struggles. Not only can they help keep you accountable, but having a support network will protect you from feeling alone. Some of the greatest Christian ministries have crashed violently because one or more of their leaders fell into sexual sin. In every case, the leader was working in some kind of isolation, either emotional or practical. I believe that if you find yourself tempted, even by pornography, you need to prayerfully throw yourself into revitalizing your Christian relationships, especially your marriage.

Finally, be practical. Admit that it is possible for you to fall into sin, and take steps to help prevent it. Don't subscribe to certain cable channels. Make it a point to travel with trusted companions. As often as you can, bring your spouse when you travel! I have found that my wife is much, much more than a safety net. She is the best spiritual partner I could imagine, and our anointings seem to grow as they flow together. Ask mentors and other trusted friends to regularly inquire about this area of your life. Avoid spending time alone with people of the opposite sex.

Remember, the anointed life is not about rules and laws, but there are things that are guaranteed to mangle your partnership with the Holy Spirit. Giving yourself guidelines will save you from God's loving discipline and from years wasted in

> YOUR SUPREME MOTIVATION: YOUR LOVE FOR JESUS.

dead religion. Above all, you should be motivated by your love for Jesus—and by His incredible love for you!

Questions for Reflection and Discussion

1. How "fresh" do you feel at this point in your life? What things seem to drag on you the most?

2. What do you do to establish healthy boundaries on your time and energies? Have you noticed whether your physical condition affects your spiritual vitality?

3. What challenges or temptations do you face that threaten to keep you from finishing well? What are you doing to protect yourself?

EPILOGUE

EPILOGUE

I hope you aren't disappointed. You may not have the emotional "pump" you've come to expect from books about reformation and the anointing. I didn't spend a lot of time telling you how to discover all your spiritual gifts and how to use them. I didn't give you a strategy for "taking your city for Jesus." (Start with a prayer walk at the McDonalds. If you can't find one, a Wendy's will do.) I just couldn't bring myself to focus on all those things, when so many foundational truths are being overlooked every day.

You do need teaching about the gifts of the Spirit. (I've made sure that my own congregation has a very well-rounded understanding.) There are other books for that. It's also true that there is much to know about organizing a citywide outreach, and it would be wise to study it out so that you don't have to reinvent the wheel. Other authors have written good books about that, and Dr. Billy Graham has refined the biblical system to something between a science and an art.

I am here—this book is here—to remind you that reformation starts with you. Before the Holy Spirit will turn your world upside down for Jesus, He wants to turn *you* upside down and inside out for Jesus! Think about it: How much of the lifestyle we've discussed comes naturally to you? Do you instinctively leap at the chance to surrender your desires to God? What do you tend to focus on—being, or doing?

Most of us find it far too easy to invest all our time into the visible things and the things that make us feel important in God's kingdom. We don't usually like to admit it, but we have the same problem Jesus' disciples did. And Jesus says to us, just as He told them,

> *You know that the rulers of the Gentiles lord it over them, and their high officials exercise authority over them. Not so with you. Instead, whoever wants to become great among you must be your servant, and whoever wants to be first must be your slave—just as the Son of Man did not come to be served, but to serve, and to give his life as a ransom for many.* (Matthew 20:25–28 NIV)

Most importantly, be patient. The anointed life is a journey. You never "arrive at" the anointing. It is something that increases as your relationship with God grows. Don't take the truths in this book for a week-long test drive and then decide that they must not work because you don't see any change. This isn't like a crash diet, where you lose twenty pounds in a week—and gain it all back in three days. This is a progressive, lifestyle kind of thing. Like a change in eating habits, it works only after you're committed to it, and even then things probably won't happen as fast as you want them to. That's okay. God's timing is never the same as our timing. That's why he saved Daniel *in* the lions' den, instead of *from* the lions' den.

Just like Daniel, you'll have a much better story if you just let God do things His way, on His schedule. You will be one of the people about whom Daniel prophesied: *"But the people that do know their God shall be strong, and do exploits"* (Daniel 11:32).

I pray that, if you get weary on your way, this book will lend you strength and encouragement. And I pray that you'll hear God's passionate heart, crying in the words of Sir Winston Churchill: "Never give up! Never give up! Never give up! Never, never, NEVER GIVE UP!"

ABOUT THE
AUTHOR

ABOUT THE AUTHOR

D r. Anthony L. Jinwright has served as Senior Pastor of Greater Salem Church for over twenty-one years. Being a man of vision, he has led Greater Salem Church to become a holistic ministry that strives to meet the total needs of individuals, the church, and community. As a result of his inspired leadership, not only have new ministries been established but Greater Salem Church is also one of the fastest growing ministries in the country.

Dr. Jinwright is being used by God to proclaim the Gospel locally, nationally, and abroad. His professional accomplishments include the following:

- Visionary Leader, North Carolina Pastors Consortium
- Board of Advisors, Gordon-Conwell Theological Seminary
- Board of Regents, The National Center for Faith-Based Initiative, West Palm Beach, Florida

- Ministered to our African brothers and sisters in South Africa

- Former Instructor and Lecturer for the Congress of Christian Education of the National Baptist Convention, U.S.A., Inc.

- Former 1st and 3rd Vice-President of the General Baptist State Convention of North Carolina, Inc.

- Former Chairman of the Evangelism Conference of the General Baptist State Convention, U.S.A., Inc.

- Owner and CEO of the A. L. Jinwright Funeral Service

Dr. Anthony L. Jinwright is also a firm believer in education and has earned several degrees as a result of his hard work and study. His educational accomplishments are:

- Gordon-Conwell Theological Seminary, Charlotte, NC, Doctor of Ministry

- Hood Theological Seminary, Livingston College, Salisbury, NC, Master of Divinity

- Trinity Theological Seminary, Newburg, IN, Master of Ministry

- Trinity College of the Bible, Newburg, IN, Bachelor of Religious Education

- American Academy McAllister Institute of Funeral Services, New York, NY, License in Mortuary Science

Dedicated to excellence, Dr. Jinwright's passion to serve transcends traditional and usual protocol. He exemplifies the character of Christ in his everyday living and service. Many look upon him with admiration and respect. His philosophy is: "The depth and height of a man can be determined by his faith and strength in God, and through his belief that he can do all things through Christ who strengthens him."

He is married to Minister Harriet Porter-Jinwright. They are the proud parents of one daughter, Anthonae LaVore Jinwright.

REFERENCES

Anderson, Ray S. 1997. *The Soul of Ministry: Forming Leaders for God's People.* Louisville, Ky.: Westminster John Knox Press.

Barna, George. 1996. *The Index of Leading Spiritual Indicators.* Dallas: Word Publishing.

———. 2002. *Growing True Disciples: New Strategies for Producing Genuine Followers of Christ.* Glendale, Calif.: Isaachar Resources.

Bianco, Margery Williams. 1991. *The Velveteen Rabbit.* New York: Delacorte Publishers.

Bounds, E. M. 1997. *E. M. Bounds on Prayer.* New Kensington, Pa.: Whitaker House.

Bromiley, Geoffrey. 1985. *The Theological Dictionary of the New Testament.* Edited by Gerhard Kittel and Gerhard Friedrich. Grand Rapids, Mich.: Wm. B. Eerdmans.

Choy, Leona F. 1990. *Powerlines: What Great Evangelicals Believed about the Holy Spirit.* Camp Hill, Pa.: Christian Publications.

Comfort, Ray. 2002. *Hell's Best Kept Secret.* New Kensington, Pa.: Whitaker House.

Dawn, Marva, and Martin E. Marty. 1995. *Reaching Out without Dumbing Down: A Theology of Worship for the Turn-of-the-Century Culture.* Grand Rapids, Mich.: Wm. B. Eerdmans.

Fee, Gordon D. 1994. *God's Empowering Presence: The Holy Spirit in the Letters of Paul.* Peabody, Mass.: Hendrickson Publishers.

Fee, Gordon D., and Douglas Stuart. 1993. *How to Read the Bible for All It Is Worth.* Grand Rapids, Mich.: Zondervan.

Finney, Charles. 1999. *Holy Spirit Revivals.* New Kensington, Pa.: Whitaker House.

———. 2000. *Power from God.* New Kensington, Pa.: Whitaker House.

Foster, Richard. 1998. *Streams of Living Water: Celebrating the Great Traditions of Christian Faith.* San Francisco: HarperCollins.

Gallup, George, Jr., and Jim Castelli. 1989. *The People's Religion: American Faith in the '90s.* New York: MacMillan Co.

Guinness, Os. 1998. *The Call.* Nashville: Word Publishing.

Kemp, A. 1997. *Seeking the Holy Spirit's Work in Expository Preaching.* Vol. 1. Doctor of Ministry Dissertation. Charlotte, N.C.: Gordon-Conwell Theological Seminary.

Kinlaw, Dennis F. 1985. *Preaching in the Spirit: A Preacher Looks for Something that Human Energy Cannot Provide.* Grand Rapids, Mich.: Francis Asbury Press.

Knox, John. 1957. *The Integrity of Preaching.* Nashville: Abingdon Press.

LaRue, Cleophus J. 2000. *The Heart of Black Preaching.* Louisville, Ky.: John Knox Press.

Lloyd-Jones, D. Martyn. 1972. *Preaching and Preachers.* Grand Rapids, Mich: Zondervan.

———. 1987. *The Puritans: Their Origins and Successors.* Philadelphia: Banner of Truth.

McFarland, Kenneth. 1961. *Eloquence in Public Speaking: How to Set Your Words on Fire.* Upper Saddle River, N.J.: Prentice Hall.

Morgenthaler, Sally. 1995. *Worship Evangelism: Inviting Unbelievers into the Presence of God.* Grand Rapids, Mich.: Zondervan.

Muck, Terry. 1985. *Liberating the Leader's Prayer Life.* Waco, Tex.: Word Publishing.

Newsboys, The. 1994. "Spirit Thing," written by Steve Taylor and Peter Furler. From the album *Going Public* by Ariose Music.

Oldford, Stephen. 1998. *Anointed Expository Preaching.* Nashville: Broadman and Holman.

Peterson, Eugene H. 1998. *The Contemplative Pastor: Returning to the Art of Spiritual Direction.* Grand Rapids, Mich.: Wm. B. Eerdmans.

Redman, Matt. 2001. *The Unquenchable Worshipper: Coming Back to the Heart of Worship.* Ventura, Ca.: Regal Books.

Robinson, Haddon. 1980. *Biblical Preaching: The Development and Delivery of Expository Messages.* Grand Rapids, Mich.: Baker Book House.

Roof, Wade Clark. 1993. *A Generation of Seekers: The Spiritual Journeys of the Baby Boom Generation.* New York: HarperCollins.

Sanders, J. Oswald. 1994. *Spiritual Leadership: Principles of Excellence for Every Believer.* Chicago: Moody Press.

Tozer, A. W. 1948. *The Pursuit of God.* Harrisburg, Pa.: Christian Publications.

ADDITIONAL SOURCES

Barnett, Paul. 1997. *The Second Epistle to the Corinthians. The New International Commentary of the New Testament.* Grand Rapids, Mich.: Wm. B. Eerdmans.

Bennis, Warren G., and Burt Nanus. 1985. *Leaders: The Strategies for Taking Charge.* New York: Harper and Row.

Blackaby, Henry, Kerry L. Skinner, and Henry Brandt. 1997. *The Power of the Call.* Nashville: Broadman and Holman.

Boyd, Gregory. 1997. *God at War: The Bible and Spiritual Conflict.* Downers Grove, Ill.: InterVarsity Press.

Broadus, John. 1979. *On the Preparation and Delivery of Sermons.* San Francisco: Harper and Row.

Brooks, P. 1964. *On Preaching.* New York: The Seabury Press.

Clements, R. September 1996. Why Preach? *Preaching Magazine.*

Craddock, Fred. 1985. *Preaching.* Nashville: Abingdon Press.

Forbes, James. 1989. *The Holy Spirit and Preaching.* Nashville: Abingdon Press.

Ford, Leighton. 1966. *The Christian Persuader.* Minneapolis, Minn.: World Wide Publications.

Larsen, David. 1999. *The Anatomy of Preaching: Identifying the Issues in Preaching Today.* Grand Rapids, Mich.: Kregel.

Lloyd-Jones, D. Martyn. 1987. *Revival.* Wheaton, Ill.: Crossway Books.

London, H. B. 1996. *Renew, Refresh, Revive.* Colorado Springs: Focus on the Family Publishing.

Macchia, Stephen. 1999. *Becoming a Healthy Church.* Grand Rapids, Mich.: Baker Book House.

Malphurs, Aubrey. 1993. *Pouring New Wine into Old Wineskins: How to Change a Church without Destroying It.* Grand Rapids, Mich.: Baker Book House.

———. 1992. *Developing a Vision for Ministry in the 21st Century.* Grand Rapids, Mich.: Baker Book House.

McKim, D. September 11, 1983. What Can We Learn from Luther the Preacher? *Christianity Today.*

Menzies, Robert. 1994. *Empowered for Witness: The Spirit in Luke–Acts.* Sheffield, England: Sheffield Academic Press.

Miller, Calvin. 1996. *Spirit, Word, and Story.* Grand Rapids, Mich.: Baker Book House.

Morgan, G. Campbell. 1937. *Preaching.* London: Marshall, Morgan, and Scott.

Northouse, Peter G. 1997. *Leadership: Theory and Practice.* London: Sage.

Penny, F. W. 1999. *Applying a Spiritual Warfare Cosmology to Preaching.* Doctor of Ministry Thesis. Charlotte, N.C.: Gordon-Conwell Theological Seminary.

Piper, John. 1990. *The Supremacy of God in Preaching.* Grand Rapids, Mich.: Baker Book House.

Sargent, T. 1994. *The Sacred Anointing: The Preaching of Dr. Martyn Lloyd-Jones.* Wheaton, Ill.: Crossway Books.

Spurgeon, Charles H. 1954. *Lectures to My Students.* Grand Rapids, Mich.: Zondervan.

Stanford, Miles J. 1981. *The Green Letters.* Grand Rapids, Mich.: Zondervan.

Stott, John R. W. 1982. *Between Two Worlds: The Art of Preaching in the 20th Century.* Grand Rapids, Mich.: Wm. B. Eerdmans.

Thrall, Bill, Bruce McNicol, and Ken McElrath. 1999. *The Ascent of a Leader: How Ordinary Relationships Develop Extraordinary Character and Influence.* San Francisco: Jossey-Bass.

Wiersbe, Warren. 1984. *Wycliffe Handbook of Preaching and Preachers.* Chicago: Moody Press.

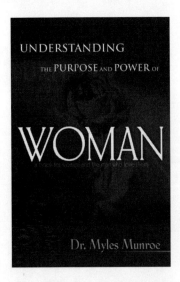

ANOTHER POWERFUL *Book*
from Whitaker House

Even with My Issues
Dr. Wanda A. Turner

The enemy will try anything to prevent you from moving beyond your issues, but you can be free of their shame and bondage. Dr. Wanda Turner invites you on the most challenging journey you will ever take—a journey from rejection to acceptance, from fear to faith, from a shattered life to wholeness. Discover how you, too, can be entirely set free.

ISBN: 0-88368-673-2 • Trade • 160 pages